ABOUT THE AUTHOR

ALAN MURRAY is the deputy managing editor of *The Wall Street Journal* and executive editor for WSJ.com and the MarketWatch Web site. Previously, he spent more than a decade as *The Wall Street Journal*'s Washington bureau chief, and during his tenure, the Washington bureau won three Pulitzer Prizes, as well as many other awards. Mr. Murray has also garnered many awards for his own writing, including two Overseas Press Club awards for his writings on Asia, a Gerald Loeb award and a John Hancock award for his coverage of the Federal Reserve, and the Society of American Business Editors and Writers "Best in Business" award for his business column. He is the author of *Revolt in the Boardroom*, *Showdown at Gucci Gulch*, and *The Wealth of Choices*.

THE WALL STREET JOURNAL.

Essential Guide to **MANAGEMENT**

Also by **ALAN MURRAY**

The Wealth of Choices
Showdown at Gucci Gulch
Revolt in the Boardroom

THE WALL STREET JOURNAL.

ESSENTIAL GUIDE TO
MANAGEMENT

• • •

Lasting Lessons from the

Best Leadership Minds

of Our Time

• • •

ALAN MURRAY

HARPER
BUSINESS

NEW YORK • LONDON • TORONTO • SYDNEY

HARPER

BUSINESS

HarperCollins books may be purchased for educational, business, or sales promotional use. For information please write: Special Markets Department, HarperCollins Publishers, 10 East 53rd Street, New York, NY 10022.

FIRST EDITION

Designed by Betty Lew

Library of Congress Cataloging-in-Publication Data

Murray, Alan.
    The Wall Street Journal essential guide to management : lasting lessons from the best leadership minds of our time / Alan Murray. — 1st ed.
        p. cm.
    Summary: "From *The Wall Street Journal* comes the definitive guide to how to be a successful manager"—Provided by publisher.
        ISBN 978-0-06-184033-3 (pbk.)
        1. Management. I. Wall Street journal (Eastern ed.) II. Title.
    III. Title: Essential guide to management.

HD31.M825 2010
658—dc22
                                                            2010002879

10 11 12 13 14 ov/RRD 10 9 8 7 6 5 4 3 2 1

CONTENTS

PREFACE

This book was written during a period of economic disruption, caused by an unprecedented financial crisis that led to the deepest economic downturn since the 1930s. During an extraordinary nine days in September 2008, the U.S. government upended the very foundations of capitalism, nationalizing Fannie Mae and Freddie Mac, arranging a shotgun marriage between Merrill Lynch and Bank of America, allowing the spectacular failure of Lehman Brothers, and then engineering a massive bailout of AIG.

In the aftermath, my neighbors in Greenwich, Connecticut, had the look of lost souls. They had built their spacious mansions and bought their costly foreign cars on the certainty that the global economy would continue to be driven by finance, and finance would continue to be dominated by the United States. As they sifted through the rubble, that certainty disappeared. Both the value of financial innovation and the dominance of American finance came into serious question. The Internet bubble had left behind a legacy of technology after it burst. Aside from Greenwich mansions and Maseratis, it was unclear what legacy the financial bubble might have left. Mortgage-backed securities? Credit default swaps? Who really needed them?

The effects weren't limited to finance. Every business, every organization, had to rethink its operations, to reflect what Ian Davis of McKinsey and Company called "the new normal." "We are experiencing not merely another turn of the business cycle," he wrote, "but a restructuring of the economic order." Debt was going to be less plentiful, government was going to be bigger and more intrusive, consumers were going to be more cautious, and business was going to have to adopt a new humility.

Uncertainty was the order of the day. Extrapolations from the past—i.e., "residential real estate prices always rise" or "postwar recessions last six to eight months"—were no longer valid. Nassim Nicholas Taleb's book *The Black Swan*, about powerful events that can neither be predicted nor explained, became the new business bible. The only certainty was that the future would look very different from the past.

It was clear we had reached the end of an era. I had gone to graduate school at the London School of Economics in 1979, just as the old era was beginning. While LSE was still a bastion of left-wing political thought, Margaret Thatcher was setting a new direction for England, extracting government from business and embracing the power of markets. At home, Ronald Reagan took office and pursued a similar course. *Privatization* and *deregulation* became the watchwords.

As the *Journal*'s economics correspondent, I had a prime seat to watch the subsequent collapse of communism. I traveled to Poland with a group of cabinet secretaries from the administration of the first President Bush, and met with Leszek Balcerowicz, the man who had been charged with the task of transforming that nation's socialist economy into a capitalist one. One of the cabinet secretaries asked Balcerowicz whether he was seeking some sort of third way—like Sweden, perhaps—to soften the transition to capitalism. Balcerowicz replied unequivocally. The cold war was over. Communism had lost. Capitalism had won. There was no third way.

At the same time, U.S. business was undergoing a glasnost of its own. In the 1950s and 1960s, analysts like John Kenneth Galbraith had found surprising parallels between America's large corporations and the Soviet Union's planning agencies. Information rose to the top. Orders flowed down. Hierarchy ruled.

By the late 1970s and 1980s, however, that was all changing. A little book called *Up the Organization: How to Stop the Corporation from Stifling People and Strangling Profits* became a runaway hit. Its author, former Avis CEO Robert Townsend, called on executives to "fire the whole advertising department," "fire the whole personnel department," and "yes, fire the PR department, too." To get rid of self-perpetuating bureaucracies, he suggested a Vice President in Charge of Killing Things. After the killing was done, he called for a new approach that empowered people, encouraged debate, delegated responsibility, and demanded excellence. Similar ideas rippled through business schools and took root at the best-managed companies.

Parallel revolutions in politics, economic policy, and management led to an extraordinary period of business creativity and prosperity. For the United States and the United Kingdom, which were at the original epicenter, it brought rejuvenation and rebirth. The prophets of decline who stood ready to write the American epitaph in the late 1970s and 1980s were forced to tear up their scripts in the 1990s and acknowledge a continued national vitality they had never imagined. Meanwhile, parts of the developing world—China and India in particular—enjoyed a burst in prosperity and the greatest alleviation of poverty that the world had ever seen.

But the pendulum always swings back. That remarkable heyday of global capitalism had already started to wear out its welcome before the crisis hit. The collapse of the Internet stock bubble, the terror attacks of September 11, and the corporate scandals at Enron, WorldCom, Adelphia, Parmalat, and more, all took their toll. Government began to reassert itself, first in matters of security, then in matters of corporate governance.

Then came September 2008—a clean break. History thereafter would be divided into neat parts—before and after. A new era had begun.

At the *Journal*, by coincidence, September 16 was the day when we launched a revamped version of our Web site, WSJ.com. The new site not only had an updated look and feel and more multimedia tools, but also, for the first time, allowed readers to comment on our stories. With such big news breaking, traffic to the Web site soared to more than twenty million visitors a month, and comments poured in.

As executive editor of the Web site, I was able to watch as both our reporters and our readers struggled to make sense of the changes buffeting them. As always, the *Journal*'s reporters led the way on many of these developments, with stories like the ones Kate Kelly wrote on the fall of Bear Stearns, or the story that Monica Langley wrote about how mighty Citigroup Inc. had been reduced to pleading with its government overseers on even minute details of its operations. Langley quoted CEO Vikram Pandit begging a senior government official: "Don't give up on us."

In November, shortly after the election of Barack Obama, the *Journal* pulled together roughly a hundred CEOs of the largest companies in the world—people like Eric Schmidt of Google, Carlos Ghosn of Nissan, Jeff Bewkes of Time Warner, Jeffrey Kindler of Pfizer, and Angela Braly of WellPoint. As host for the event, I was able to listen in on their private debates as they struggled with some of the biggest issues facing both business and government—the future of the economy and the financial system, the challenges of the health care system, the need to move away from dependence on carbon-based fuels. After the meeting, many of the CEOs provided additional counsel as I continued the work on this book.

What struck me about this extraordinary period in our history was the degree to which it validated the need for better management. For some time, management experts had emphasized the creation of organizations that had less hierarchy, were more open and flexible, more democratic, that had distributed decision-making structures, and that were prepared to deal with rapid and unexpected change. These were exactly the characteristics that had allowed the best-managed firms to ride out the crisis, and their absence is what caused others to fail.

The firms that survived—I think of Dick Kovacevich's Wells Fargo—did so because they were organized to deal with the unexpected. They were managed by people who insisted on a culture of candor, and who didn't let fancy risk models cloud their basic judgment and common sense.

Watching the chaotic aftermath of the crisis convinced me that the need for this book was greater than ever. Managers everywhere are in uncharted waters. They are looking for navigation guides.

In what follows, I hope we have provided them with one.

—ALAN MURRAY
December 2009

Management is not about doing easy things. Management is about doing things that, usually, people don't want to do.

—CARLOS GHOSN, *CEO, Nissan Motor Corporation, in a video interview for* The Wall Street Journal*'s Lessons in Leadership series*

THE WALL STREET JOURNAL.

Essential Guide to **MANAGEMENT**

INTRODUCTION

Every day, every hour, hundreds of people with no particular training or education or demonstrated aptitude for the job, are made managers.

They may have been superb software engineers or gold-star salespeople or even brilliant journalists. But now, suddenly, they are being asked to do a job that is entirely foreign to their experience. It's as if the airlines chose their pilots from among their passengers.

Wait a minute, you say. Managing isn't like flying an airplane. It's intuitive. It's people skills—the sort you've been honing since you entered nursery school. You don't need hours of in-flight training to do the job. You just need to follow your gut.

Well, you might think that. But you'd be wrong. Your intuition, your "gut," will often lead you astray in the field of management. Learning from those who've gone before you, or who've watched and studied the successes and failures of those who've gone before, could prove critical to your success.

The last century has seen an explosion in the study of management practices. Management guru Peter Drucker called it "the most important innovation of the twentieth century." And among serious students, that study has led to a surprising degree of consensus on which management practices get good results, and which get bad ones.

Yet in spite of that studied consensus, the world is overflowing with managers who embrace the worst and ignore the best. All of us can tell horror stories about the bad management practices we encounter in our daily lives. We can relate to the experiences of the cartoon character Dilbert, whose pointy-headed boss charts his course by spinning a wheel with four basic strategies: "Reorganize," "Yell," "Be Unclear," and "Hide." And we appreciate the humor in the successful TV series *The Office*, where bad management is raised to an art.

The Office first aired in England on the BBC in 2001. The U.S. version began in 2005, with comedian Steve Carell cast in the lead as Michael Scott, the Scranton, Pennsylvania, regional manager of the Dunder Mifflin paper company.

In the show, Scott frequently launches into soliloquies about the importance of leadership. He sees himself as an enlightened manager, throwing parties and hosting the annual "Dundee" awards to motivate his employees. The most important thing about the company, he propounds, "is the people."

But in truth he is petty, dictatorial, indecisive, insensitive, and timid—the antithesis of the successful manager. He doesn't like firing employees, or cutting their benefits, so he delegates those tasks to his sadistic assistant, Dwight Schrute, who is more than eager to take them on. He shows no awareness of the larger problems facing his firm—an independent paper company struggling to survive in the face of competition from the likes of Staples, Office Depot, and OfficeMax. And he seems to have no ability to inspire any emotion in his employees, other than despair.

"Right now, this is just a job," says Jim Halpert, the unassuming hero of the series. "If I advance any higher in this company, then this would be my career. And, well, if this were my career, I'd have to throw myself in front of a train."

The series struck a chord, in large part because the antics inside

Dunder Mifflin are so familiar. Bad management has become a pervasive and recognizable part of everyday life.

New managers, in particular, get it wrong. They go into their jobs thinking, like Michael Scott, that they are in charge. Instead, they find their actions constrained in every direction: by overbearing bosses, by needy and crafty employees, by a vast network of colleagues and suppliers and customers on whom they depend but over whom they have little control. Caught unawares, the new manager can spend all day, every day, responding to the endless demands of others.

"Becoming a manager is not about becoming a boss; it's about becoming a hostage," one recently promoted manager told Harvard Business School professor Linda Hill.

New managers think their authority comes from their title and position. They expect employees to do as they are told. Instead, they find direct orders are ignored or avoided; moreover, the most talented employees are often least likely to obey. In response, the new manager may attempt to demand absolute obeisance to every request . . . only to find disaster ensues.

And like Michael Scott, new managers often try to befriend their employees, then find that every new friendship becomes a source of controversy with others and undermines the group's ability to work as a team.

It doesn't have to be that way. At its best, management is the stuff that has enabled many of humanity's greatest successes. It enables us to harness the efforts and skills and knowledge of dozens or hundreds or even thousands of people and keep them focused on a greater goal. Good management is a noble endeavor—it enables us to be part of something much larger than ourselves.

In recent decades, some of the world's best and brightest have devoted countless hours to understanding management, what works, and what doesn't. There are more than 1,500 credible schools offering master's degrees in business administration around the world, nearly a hundred magazines and newspapers devoted to the subject, and more than three thousand new books on the topic each year. Many of the books are quite good.

But who has the time? Especially if, as is often the case, you've been asked to take on this new challenge tomorrow. What's missing isn't sufficient learning or understanding of management techniques. What's missing is a simple and convenient way of disseminating that understanding to a group of people who, by definition, lead very busy lives. What's missing is a simple, easy guide to the best management practices.

The Wall Street Journal Essential Guide to Management is our attempt to fill that void.

I have been a manager, in some form, for more than three decades. But this book isn't based solely, or even primarily, on my own experience. Nor does it attempt to propound some novel theory of management.

Rather, this book is an effort to draw the best from the existing body of knowledge, research, and practice, and to summarize it in one place, in a simple, clear, and useful way. If you are a new manager, or even an experienced manager who worries your methods bear a striking similarity to those of Michael Scott, you'll want to read this book from beginning to end. Others may choose to use it as a resource or reference. It is organized by topics and addresses the questions most frequently asked by managers. For those who wish to dive deeper, I've offered suggestions for further reading with each topic.

In preparation for this task, I have read dozens of the best books on management, as well as numerous articles and papers. I have tried to focus on the authors who are frequently cited as influential in the field—people like Peter Drucker, Michael Porter, Clayton Christensen,

Tom Peters, Gary Hamel, John Kotter, Jim Collins, Jack Welch, and Larry Bossidy, to name a few. I've also used those books that have resonated with the broadest audiences—books like *Who Moved My Cheese?*, by Spencer Johnson, and *The Seven Habits of Highly Effective People*, by Stephen Covey.

Where possible, I've relied on hard evidence, not just folk wisdom or anecdote. In their excellent book *Hard Facts*, Jeffrey Pfeffer and Robert Sutton of Stanford University argue that business advice is often based on loose use, or even misuse, of anecdotes. "Suppose you went to a doctor who said, 'I'm going to do an appendectomy on you.' When you ask why, the doctor answers, 'Because I did one on my last patient and it made him better.'" Too much management advice follows that same logic.

Most important, I've also been able to draw on the experience and expertise of my colleagues at *The Wall Street Journal*, who have had front row seats for many of the great management dramas of recent years. For any serious student of management, nothing matches the *Journal*'s broad reach and authority on these subjects.

Through the reporting of Mike Miller and Laurie Hays, for example, readers were able to watch one of the great management stories of recent decades: Louis Gerstner's turnaround of IBM, from a stodgy, white-shirt seller of mainframe computers, to a nimble, modern technology company.

Miller and Hays were there when Gerstner made his surprising pronouncement: "The last thing IBM needs is a vision"—a comment that symbolized for a generation that *strategy* without *execution* is pointless. They watched as the famously rigid IBM culture rebelled against Gerstner's attempts to change it, and his decision to toss out the three "basic beliefs" propounded by the revered Thomas Watson Jr., son of the company's founder.

And they watched as Gerstner's changes slowly began to take hold, saving the iconic company from slipping into obscurity, like Westing-house, RCA, or other great companies of the past that never made it to the future.

IBM was a success story. But *Journal* reporters have also watched failure up close . . . like "Chainsaw Al" Dunlap's meltdown at appliance maker Sunbeam.

A graduate of West Point, Dunlap earned his stripes—and the name "Rambo in Pinstripes"—by shedding thousands of workers at troubled companies like Scott Paper and Crown Zellerbach. He professed to work only for the shareholders—showing little sympathy or understanding of his employees or, for that matter, even his customers. Shareholders rewarded him by cheering him on and driving up the stock price of any company he came near.

But *Journal* colleagues including Thomas Petzinger, Robert Frank, and Joann Lublin were there when the man's arrogance caught up with him. While running Sunbeam, he trumpeted his own successes in a book called *Mean Business* and agreed to pose for a photo in bandoliers and pistols. Those tin-eared gestures were indication enough that for "Chainsaw Al," it was all about him, not about the companies he was running.

The directors of Sunbeam Corp. eventually figured that out, and in June of 1998, they tossed him out of the job.

There are lessons in these stories, and many more like them, that have appeared in the *Journal* over the years. This book attempts to assemble the most important of those lessons in one place.

For additional guidance, I've also relied on the members of *The Wall Street Journal* CEO Council—an elite group of chief executives of large and successful global companies who have learned a good deal about leadership and management on their way to the top. Among other things, I asked the group to suggest the best books they've read on management and have incorporated their suggestions throughout. The *Journal* also did video interviews with many members of this council on key management topics, and I've included excerpts of those interviews where appropriate throughout the book.

A warning: you'll find no gimmicks in these pages. No "one-minute" methods. No animal parables. No money-back guarantees. I've attempted to be clear, but at the same time to avoid oversimplification.

What you will find, I hope, is distilled wisdom and learning. When you finish this book, you'll have seen modern management at work, and you'll have been exposed to the best management thinking and advice currently available.

What you do then is up to you.

A note on the organization of this book.

Chapter One—Management starts with the basics: what is a manager, and how has the job changed in recent years. That chapter states a central thesis of this book—that to be a good manager in today's workplace, you must also be a good leader.

Chapter Two—Leadership deals with different leadership styles, and what works best in the workplace. This chapter emphasizes that a key to leadership is understanding what motivates the people you are attempting to lead.

Chapter Three Motivation explores the fundamental question: Why do people work? Having a clear understanding of the answer is critical to being a good leader and a good manager.

Chapter Four—People is about building your team—hiring, firing, evaluating, and ensuring your employees are engaged in their work.

Chapter Five—Strategy deals with a key responsibility of the manager—figuring out where you are heading, and how you intend to get there. It's the manager's job to make sure the group has a clear *mission*, a *strategy* for achieving that vision, and clear *goals* to be met along the way.

Chapter Six—Execution is about the day-to-day task of implementing your vision, strategy, and goals. How do you get an organization to follow the path that's been set for it, and how do you keep it from veering off course, or stalling along the way? This chapter includes the essentials of running a high performance organization.

Chapter Seven—Teams deals with what's become the central unit of modern organizational life. The complexity of the modern world means many tasks require cross-functional teamwork. As a manager, you'll often find you can't accomplish ambitious goals without the help of people who don't directly report to you. That requires a different set of skills, which we will outline.

Chapter Eight—Change is about the challenges of operating in a rapidly changing environment—an inescapable aspect of modern management. This chapter also looks at the future of management, and how it may have to adapt to deal with rapid change.

Chapter Nine—Financial Literacy is about using the financial tools you'll need to keep your organization on track. If you don't master them, they may master you.

Chapter Ten—Going Global looks at some of the unique challenges that operating in a global economy pose to the modern manager.

Chapter Eleven—Ethics focuses on the importance of doing good even as you are doing well.

Chapter Twelve—You is about taking care of number one. Organizations are no longer paternalistic, if they ever really were, and modern managers have to assume they won't work at the same place their entire working lives. That makes managing yourself and your relations and your personal *brand* increasingly important.

So jump in. The answers aren't quite as easy as some quickie management schemes suggest. But truth is, they aren't all that difficult either. At its core, being a good manager is about being an effective person. The lessons you learn here can help you throughout your life.

Sometimes when you are a leader, you have this pressure to be a motivator. And the pressure to be a motivator could lead you to be a little more optimistic than you should otherwise be. I think the best thing is to call things the way they are. . . .

When I joined Kodak, we had manufacturing plants for film all over the world. A lot of those plants needed to be shut down. And I would go to some of those places and before I would even say my name, I'd say "Would you please stand up if you have a digital camera in your household?" And 40 or 50 percent would stand up. And I'd say, "I'm Antonio Perez. I'm your new leader. And obviously we have a problem here. If we aren't going to buy film, who is?"

ANTONIO PEREZ, *CEO, Kodak,*
in a video interview for The Wall Street Journal's
Lessons in Leadership series

Chapter ONE

MANAGEMENT

What is a manager?

In simplest terms, a manager is someone who organizes a group of people to accomplish a goal. It is a job as old as the human race. But as society has become more complex, the job of the manager has become ever more essential.

Indeed it's impossible to imagine what life would be like without managers. Individual genius may be at the source of many of humanity's great innovations. But turning those innovations into products and services that can widely benefit mankind is the function of management. Without it, we would still be living in the Stone Age.

As an academic discipline, management is much younger. Frederick Winslow Taylor is often cited as the founder of management studies. His 1911 book, *The Principles of Scientific Management*, portrays managers as organizers: they arranged the cogs in the great industrial machine. Their job was all about increasing efficiency and productivity, in order to get workers the one thing they most wanted—high wages—while also delivering to owners the thing they most needed—low labor costs. For Taylor, management "studies" meant standing in a workplace with a stopwatch, measuring each action taken by the workers, and devising ways to eliminate "all false movements, slow movements and useless movements." For several generations of managers who followed him, the goal remained the same: organizing factories and workplaces so that the same group of people working the same hours could produce ever more products.

But in the years since World War II, the nature of work has changed. Peter Drucker was the first to clearly capture the difference. A native of Vienna, Austria, Drucker had worked as a journalist and studied economics as a young man. At some point in his studies, he had an epiphany. Economists, he realized, "were interested in the behavior of commodities, while I was interested in the behavior of people." And people behaved very differently than commodities. Any theory, whether of economics or of management, that posited human beings as uniform and replaceable inputs in a great industrial machine was fundamentally flawed.

That epiphany became the foundation of modern management.

In 1959, Drucker became the first to use the phrase "knowledge worker"—a term that referred to people whose work primarily involves the manipulation of information and knowledge, rather than manual labor. The knowledge worker's contribution to an enterprise couldn't be measured with a stopwatch or a punch card. It couldn't be forced or controlled by any amount of oversight. And it couldn't be encouraged by simple pay schemes tied to hourly output.

In Taylor's world, management was about four things: *planning, organizing, directing, monitoring.* In Drucker's world, however, *motivating* talented knowledge workers to give their most became a broader challenge. He broke down being a manager into five pieces. A manager, he wrote:

Sets objectives—He or she is responsible for determining what the overall objective of the group is, sets goals for each member of the group, and decides what needs to be done to reach those goals and objectives.

Organizes—He or she divides the work into achievable chunks and decides who must do what.

Motivates and communicates—The manager creates a team out of the workers, so that they can work together smoothly toward a common goal.

Measures—The manager creates yardsticks and targets and determines whether they are achieved.

Finally, a manager *develops people.* In Drucker's world, people aren't interchangeable cogs; they are individuals who must be trained and developed in order to achieve the full power of the organization.

Drucker's insights into motivating workers are the foundation of modern management studies and lead to a central thesis of this book: to be a good manager in today's world, you must also be a good leader of people.

"One does not 'manage' people," Drucker concluded from his observations. "The task is to lead them." The manager of people has to be a motivator of people. It is not enough to give employees directions. Managers must give their employees more—they must give them purpose.

What exactly does that mean? In his 1989 book, *On Becoming a Leader*, Warren Bennis compiled a long list of the differences between managers and leaders. Among them:

- The manager administers; the leader innovates.
- The manager focuses on systems and structure; the leader focuses on people.
- The manager relies on control; the leader inspires trust.
- The manager has a short-range view; the leader has a long-range perspective.
- The manager asks how and when; the leader asks what and why.

- The manager has his or her eye always on the bottom line; the leader's eye is on the horizon.
- The manager imitates; the leader originates.
- The manager accepts the status quo; the leader challenges it.
- The manager is the classic good soldier; the leader is his or her own person.
- The manager does things right; the leader does the right thing.

The challenge for the modern manager—and the reason why being a modern manager has become such a challenge—is that you must do *all of the above*. In the best managed organizations, you will be expected to administer *and* innovate; to focus on systems, structure, *and* people; to exercise control as well as extend trust; to watch both the short-term and the long-term. To be successful as a manager in today's world, you'll have to be prepared to ask all four questions—how, when, what, and why. You'll have to keep one eye on the bottom line and one eye on the horizon. You'll be expected not only to take orders, but also to challenge the status quo when necessary. It will be your responsibility not only to do things right, but also to make sure you and your organization are doing the right things. It's an awesome task. But as this book will show, it's essential. Managing without leading is a recipe for failure.

And by the way, attempting to lead without actually managing is disastrous as well. Many managers have met their downfall by setting an ambitious vision for their organization, and then assuming someone else would execute that vision.

"I'm all for dreaming," writes Stanford professor Robert Sutton in a blog post on this subject. "And some of the most unlikely and impressive things have been done by dreamers. But one characteristic of the successful dreamers I think of—Francis Ford Coppola, Steve Jobs—is that they also have a remarkably deep understanding of the industry they work in and the people they lead, and they often are willing to get very deep in the weeds. This ability to go back and forth between the little details and the big picture is also evident in the behavior of some of the leaders I admire most," he says, mentioning Anne Mulcahy, former CEO of Xerox, Bill George, former CEO of Medtronic, and Mark Hurd, CEO of Hewlett-Packard.

Allan Cohen, dean of Babson College's School of Business, makes a similar point. "Leaders who don't understand how the organization works can't lead very well. Managers who don't have any notion of where they might be headed don't last very long anymore."

These fundamental truths don't apply to just big-name, big-company CEOs like Jobs or Mulcahy or Hurd. They also apply to the millions of so-called middle managers who make up the core of any large organization.

The U.S. Census classifies about 8 percent of the workforce—or twelve million people—as "managers." Other studies have found nearly one-fifth of today's U.S. workforce—or closer to thirty million people—supervise others as a major part of their job. These people are the heart of today's organizations. In many ways, the middle manager is the great organizational success story of the last century. As organizations have become more complex, as information technology has improved, and as the speed of change has accelerated, old hierarchies have broken down. By necessity, decision making can no longer be concentrated at the top of the pyramid. It has been pushed down into the organization—to the middle managers.

Middle managers, of course, are not masters of their own fate. Unlike a Mulcahy or a Hurd or a Jobs, they must carry out an agenda that someone else has set for them. They may bear a heavy load of responsibility, but they have limited room for freedom of action. Their jobs can often be grueling and frustrating.

A decade ago, the *Journal*'s Jonathan Kaufman captured the challenges of modern middle management by shadowing the manager of an Au Bon Pain bakery café named Richard Thibeault. The forty-six-year-old Mr. Thibeault, a former factory worker, had always thought becoming a "manager" would mean he had arrived in the world. He would sit behind a desk, work nine to five, and be a pillar of the community.

Instead, he found he had to rise each day at 3 A.M. to bake muffins, prepare soups, and fret over his store's falling sales. Instead of the steady hours he enjoyed in the factory, he often put in as many as seventy hours a week. His job was an odd mix of broad responsibility and limited authority. He trimmed staff in order to meet corporate cost-cutting targets but was not allowed to cut prices in order to attract needed customers.

"Some days I think maybe I should go back to factory work," he told Kaufman. "It was easier."

Yet for all their frustrations, middle managers in today's well-run organizations often find they are given surprising responsibilities. They may find themselves heading up a team whose tasks involve not just following orders, but also solving a knotty problem or developing a new product. They will be asked to innovate, to challenge the status quo. They will be asked to use their judgment, not just to do things right, but also to make sure the organization is doing the right things.

Along the way, today's middle managers often find themselves heading projects that involve others who don't directly report to them. In these situations, giving orders, military-style, doesn't cut it. Middle managers, even more than their CEO employers, must learn to exercise influence without clear authority.

They must learn, in other words, to be leaders—the topic of our next chapter.

MANAGEMENT in Brief

- Good managers must also be good leaders.
- The modern manager must answer not only "how" and "when," but also "what" and "why."
- A good manager can't simply accept the status quo; he or she must be willing to challenge it.

Further Reading

The Principles of Scientific Management, by Frederick Winslow Taylor, 1911. Republished by NuVision Publications, LLC, 2007. This little book is an interesting read for purely historical reasons, to understand the early days of management studies.

Management, by Peter F. Drucker, HarperCollins, 1973, revised 2008. It's remarkable how well Drucker's insights about management have held up over time. This book is more than five hundred pages long, and not always easy reading. But many of the "discoveries" of subsequent management gurus can be found right here.

On Becoming a Leader, by Warren Bennis, 1989. Revised edition, Basic Books, 2003. Bennis was one of the first scholars to write about leadership; he's still one of the best.

The Truth about Middle Managers, by Paul Osterman, Harvard Business Press, 2009. Osterman wrote this book in part as an antidote to the tendency of his fellow business scholars to always focus on the challenges facing big company CEOs, a small and unrepresentative subset of the world's managers.

Random Acts of Management: A Dilbert Book, by Scott Adams, Andrews McMeel Publishing LLC, 2000. *Dilbert* should be required reading for all managers. An amusing guide to what *not* to do as a manager.

I was an ROTC person. . . . On my day to manage the brigade, at the end of the day the major said: "Cadet Morris, you had a very good day today." So I turned around to tell the team, "Gentlemen, we had an outstanding day today." And he spun around on his heels and said, "I didn't say outstanding. I said you had a good day."

He had been as tough as anyone I'd ever seen . . . the expectations were incredible. As our time together got longer, he got softer. And the lesson I took from that is you can never be soft in the early stage, and then turn hard. But you can always be a high-demand leader, and then over time . . . soften your approach.

MICHAEL MORRIS, *CEO, American Electric Power, in a video interview for* The Wall Street Journal's *Lessons in Leadership series*

Chapter **TWO**

LEADERSHIP

When you think about great leaders in history, is it a George S. Patton who comes to your mind—the outspoken general who was once relieved of command for slapping a soldier recuperating in a hospital?

Or are you more likely to think of Abraham Lincoln—quiet, thoughtful, tortured to the edge of mental illness by his own doubts?

Is it the dictatorial Julius Caesar who is your model? Or the inquisitive Socrates? Do you fashion yourself as the next "Chainsaw Al" Dunlap? Or do you relate to the unassuming Sam Walton?

Leaders, it's clear, come in all shapes, sizes, and styles. They are an indispensable part of our social fabric. They give our lives direction and meaning. "A new leader," writes Warren Bennis, "has to be able to change an organization that is dreamless, soulless and visionless."

They accomplish that in many different ways. But the question that has to be asked is: Do some ways work better than others? Is there a "right" way to lead an organization?

For years, business schools steered clear of this question. It seemed too soft and squishy—rooted in human emotions, and not measurable or quantifiable or subject to the methods of science. Business students would learn to analyze spreadsheets; but if they wanted to learn about leadership, they would have to search elsewhere. When we asked Time Warner CEO Jeff Bewkes, a Stanford Business School graduate, to name the most influential management books he has read, he bypassed business books and instead cited James Flexner's four-volume biography of George Washington. Russell Fradin, CEO of Hewitt Associates, cited Doris Kearns Goodwin's book about Abraham Lincoln, *Team of Rivals*.

In recent years, however, business schools have wised up. They've belatedly acknowledged that the fundamentals of leadership are too important to ignore. They've taken up the challenge, and retooled their programs with an eye on leadership. And from their work, as well as the work of my colleagues at *The Wall Street Journal*, you can begin to see some common traits of successful leaders.

Generalizations in this area, of course, are fraught with peril. For every rule, there is likely to be a prominent exception. Still, if there is one strong conclusion that emerges from the best work on leadership, it is this: great leaders exhibit a paradoxical mix of arrogance and humility.

Leaders must be arrogant enough to believe they are worth following, but humble enough to know that others may have a better sense of the direction they should take. They must be confident enough to inspire confidence in others, yet always open to the questions and doubts that will inevitably come their way. They must believe in themselves, but be willing to put the organization's needs above their own.

Often it's in the humility department that modern leaders fail. Witness the previously mentioned example of Chainsaw Al Dunlap, with his bandoliers and pistols. He was clearly more interested in his own image than in the success of the company he was running. Or think of Carly Fiorina, who as CEO of Hewlett-Packard had her own picture inserted on the wall between those of the company's iconic founders, Messers. Hewlett and Packard. Ms. Fiorina's leadership of H-P foundered in part because she was perceived as devoting too much time to cultivating her own image, and too little to fixing the company's internal management problems.

One of the most influential business books of recent years is Jim Collins's *Good to Great*, cited by several members of *The Wall Street Journal*'s CEO Council as the best management book they've read. "A few years ago, I was at a bookstore with my daughter and picked up a copy," says Timken Company CEO James Griffith. "I soon found a comfortable chair, and what turned out to be my all-time favorite business book."

Collins's findings on leadership are compelling in part because they were unexpected. Collins and his team launched a huge research project looking at 1,435 large companies and ultimately identifying just eleven that had made the leap from good results to great results, and then sustained those results for at least fifteen years. The team examined the good-to-great companies in relation to a comparison group, to see what made them special.

In the early stages of the project, Collins, who was inclined to believe that the importance of leadership was overstated, urged his team to "ignore the executives." But he says the team kept pushing back, saying there was something consistently unusual about the leaders of the good-to-great companies.

"We were surprised, shocked really, to discover the type of leadership required for turning a good company into a great one," Collins writes. "Compared to high-profile leaders with big personalities who make headlines and become celebrities, the good-to-great leaders seem to have come from Mars. Self-effacing, quiet, reserved, even shy—these leaders are a paradoxical blend of personal humility and professional will. They are more like Lincoln and Socrates than Patton or Caesar."

Collins did his research in the late 1990s—a time when CEOs were seeing their salaries skyrocket and were often treated with media adulation. Three CEOs were honored with *Time* magazine's "Person of the Year" award during that decade. The CEO was seen as savior— often someone who parachuted in from the outside to save a company headed on the road to ruin.

Yet Collins's "good-to-great" CEOs were people you've likely never heard of—people like Darwin Smith, who took the helm of Kimberly-Clark paper company in 1971, or Colman Mockler, CEO of Gillette from 1975 to 1991. For the most part, they grew up inside their companies rather than being brought in from the outside. A common characteristic was their profound humility—and a tendency to use the pronoun "we," not "I."

These leaders, which Collins calls "Level 5" leaders, "channel their ego needs away from themselves and into the larger goal of building a great company. It's not that Level 5 leaders have no ego or self-interest. Indeed, they are incredibly ambitious—*but their ambition is first and foremost for the institution, not themselves.*" Level 5 leaders, Collins found, created institutions that could continue to thrive after they were gone. In the comparison companies, by contrast, leaders who were "concerned more with their own reputation for personal greatness . . . often failed to set the company up for success in the next generation."

Successful succession planning, it turns out, is one of the most telling signs of a great leader. Former General Electric CEO Jack Welch distinguished himself by developing a roster of leaders who were ready to replace him when he retired. But other CEOs appear unwilling to contemplate the organization's existence after they depart. Seemingly great leaders like former Citigroup CEO Sandy Weill and former AIG CEO Hank Greenberg left behind weak legacies of leadership that ultimately undermined their organizations.

Humility alone, of course, is not enough to make a great leader. Equally important is ferocious resolve—an almost stoic determination to do whatever needs to be done to make the organization great. And that determination is often accompanied by a toughness and even ruthlessness in pursuit of goals.

Former ExxonMobil CEO Lee Raymond, for instance, was a shy, almost reclusive man when it came to personal matters. A *Journal* profile noted that when he was testifying at the trial over the *Exxon Valdez* oil spill he was asked about his own background. He responded: "I hope this doesn't get too boring. It kind of bores me." Born in the small town of Watertown, South Dakota, the son of a railroad engineer, Raymond was helping manage the family farm by age ten. He excelled in math and science in high school, studied chemical engineering, and earned his Ph.D. from the University of Minnesota before joining Exxon.

Tall, heavyset, and with a harelip, he was not an obvious choice for leadership. But his sheer determination and perseverance impressed others, and he quickly rose in the company.

As CEO, Raymond avoided public appearances in his industry. He seldom gave speeches or even met with outsiders. But he was relentless in eliminating redundant layers of management. He focused on profitability and turned ExxonMobil into the most profitable oil company in the world.

Procter & Gamble's former CEO A.G. Lafley is another example of a leader whose success reflected that paradoxical mix of arrogance and humility. Lafley inherited a company whose culture was criticized for being too insular. He single-handedly changed that culture, in part by insisting company executives spend more time with their customers. Lafley himself would make ten or fifteen such visits with consumers every year, observing women doing everything from washing clothes to applying makeup.

Journal reporter Sarah Ellison accompanied Lafley on a visit to Venezuela, where he sat in the cramped kitchen of twenty-nine-yearold Maria Yolanda Rios and listened to her talk about how often she washes her hair, what kind of skin cream she uses, and whether she uses nail polish. A housekeeper, Ms. Rios and her husband together earn just under $600 a month. But when asked to bring her beauty products into the kitchen, she returned with thirty-one bottles of cream, lotion, shampoo, and perfume.

"It's her entertainment," Lafley said. "We need to remember that."

In the process of opening up the company, Lafley also saved the iconic consumer products maker from a downward spiral.

Raymond and Lafley typify business leaders who work relentlessly on behalf of their organizations, not just themselves. They were both hugely ambitious, but their ambitions seemed as much for their companies as for their own careers.

Other modern-day business leaders have tended to put their own interests ahead of those of the organization—and suffered as a result. In 2000, for instance, the *Journal* profiled the restless Joseph Galli in his relentless quest to earn a top CEO post.

Galli worked for nineteen years at the Black & Decker Corporation and advanced to the number two spot before being forced out after failing to win the top job. He entertained offers from both PepsiCo, to run its Frito-Lay unit, and Amazon, to be number two, flip-flopping several times and embarrassing Pepsi by rejecting its offer at the last minute. His tenure at Amazon lasted only thirteen months. He was criticized for cutting staff without regard to tenure and destroying the company's "family atmosphere."

Like Raymond and Lafley, Galli was a hard driver. But unlike them, he was seen as driving to his own destination, not leading the organization to a common goal. (After a year of unemployment and self-reflection, Galli was given a chance to redeem himself, as CEO of Techtronic Industries Co., a Hong Kong–based manufacturer.)

If humility and will are the root of great leadership, they are, of course, only the root. There is much more to this complex job. In an earlier business classic, *In Search of Excellence*, Thomas Peters and

Robert Waterman Jr. made an effort to sum up the many responsibilities of leaders in a single paragraph. It's well worth careful reading:

> Leadership is many things. It is patient, usually boring coalition building. It is the purposeful seeding of cabals that one hopes will result in the appropriate ferment in the bowels of the organization. It is meticulously shifting the attention of the institution through the mundane language of management systems. It is altering agendas so that new priorities get enough attention. It is being visible when things are going awry, and invisible when they are working well. It's building a loyal team at the top that speaks more or less with one voice. It's listening carefully much of the time, frequently speaking with encouragement, and reinforcing words with believable action. It's being tough when necessary, and it's the occasional naked use of power—or the "subtle accumulation of nuances, a hundred things done a little better," as Henry Kissinger once put it.

LEADERSHIP STYLES

By now, you're beginning to understand why business educators have such a tough time teaching leadership. It's a big, vague, amorphous topic. We can write about great leaders at great length. But practically speaking, how do you become one?

A good start is to focus on leadership styles. Daniel Goleman, who popularized the notion of "emotional intelligence," has described the following six different styles that leaders use to motivate others. Our view is these are not mutually exclusive. You don't need to adopt one and ignore the others. Rather, the best leaders move among these styles, using the one that meets the needs of the moment. Think of them all as part of your management repertoire.

Visionary. This style is most appropriate when an organization needs a new direction. Its goal is to move people toward a new set of shared dreams. "Visionary leaders articulate where a group is going, but not how it will get there—setting people free to innovate, experiment, take calculated risks," writes Goleman.

Coaching. This one-on-one style focuses on developing individuals, showing them how to improve their performance, and helping to connect their goals to the goals of the organization. Coaching works best with employees who show initiative and want more professional development. But it can backfire if it's perceived as "micromanaging" an employee and undermines his or her self-confidence.

Affiliative. This style emphasizes the importance of teamwork, and creates harmony in a group by connecting people to one another. It's particularly valuable when you need to improve team harmony, increase morale, and repair communication or broken trust in an organization. But it has its drawbacks. An excessive emphasis on group praise can allow poor performance to go uncorrected and lead employees to believe that mediocrity will be tolerated.

Democratic. This style draws on people's knowledge and skills, and creates a group commitment to the resulting goals. It works best when the direction the organization should take is unclear, and the leader needs to tap the collective wisdom of the group. The consensus-building approach can be disastrous in times of crisis, however, when urgent events demand quick decisions.

Pacesetting. In this style, the leader sets high standards for performance. He or she is obsessive about doing things better and faster, and asks the same of everyone. But Goleman warns this style should be used sparingly, because it can undercut morale and make people feel as if they are failing. "Our data shows that, more often than not, pacesetting poisons the climate," he writes.

Commanding. This is classic model of "military" style leadership—probably the most often used, it is the least-often effective. Because it rarely involves praise and frequently employs criticism, it can undercut morale and job satisfaction. Still, in crisis situations, when an urgent turnaround is needed, it can be an effective approach.

Note that what distinguishes each leadership style above is not the personal characteristics of the leader, but rather the nature and needs of those who are being led. As James MacGregor Burns argued in his path-breaking 1978 book, *Leadership*: "Leadership over human beings is exercised when persons with certain motives and purposes mobilize, in competition or conflict with others, institutional, political, psychological and other resources so as to arouse, engage and satisfy the motives of followers."

Unlike "naked power wielding," he writes, "leadership is thus inseparable from followers' needs and goals."

The good leader, in other words, must understand what motivates those he or she wishes to lead—the subject of our next chapter.

LEADING IN A CRISIS

The ultimate test of leadership comes in times of crisis. That's when the rules suddenly change and most people lose their bearings. More than ever, they look to find someone who can show them a way out.

In March 2009, as the economic effects of the global financial crisis were hitting with full force, business guru Bill George laid out seven rules for leaders dealing with a crisis in an article in *The Wall Street Journal*. George, a former CEO of Medtronic, now teaches at Harvard Business School. He serves on the boards of directors of Exxon-Mobil, Goldman Sachs, and Novartis and has written one of the most popular business books of recent times, *True North*. His seven rules:

1. **Leaders must face reality.** You'll hear this theme repeatedly throughout this book, but it is never more important than in a crisis, when reality is rapidly heading south and the human tendency is always to hope the worst is over. "Reality starts with the person in charge," George writes. "Attempting to find short-term fixes that address the symptoms of the crisis only ensures the organization will wind up back in the same predicament."

2. **No matter how bad things are, they will get worse.** This is the corollary to the first rule. Faced with such bad news, many people are compelled to believe things can't get worse. They can. Far better to anticipate the worst and "get out in front of it," George says, than to adopt solutions that are too timid.

3. **Build a mountain of cash.** For business leaders, preparing for the worst means making sure you have enough cash to survive the direst circumstances.

4. **Get the world off your shoulders.** In a crisis, many leaders tend to take the problems on themselves, and try to find a solution on their own. George's advice: now more than ever, you need the help of your best people. Bring them into your confidence, get their advice, and secure their commitment for making the painful changes ahead.

5. **Before asking others to sacrifice, first volunteer yourself.** If there are sacrifices to be made, the leaders "should step up and show they will make the greatest sacrifices themselves," George says. In a crisis, everyone is watching.

6. **Never waste a crisis.** White House Chief of Staff Rahm Emmanuel used this line at *The Wall Street Journal*'s CEO Council; George attributes it to Israeli leader Benjamin Netanyahu. Many leaders have discovered its truth: a crisis creates an opportunity to gain broad support for tough actions that might not have been possible absent a crisis.

7. **Be aggressive in the marketplace.** Every crisis is also an opportunity. When others are losing their nerve, good leaders know they have a chance to prove their stuff.

LEADERSHIP in Brief

- Great leaders are a paradoxical mix of personal humility and professional will, more Lincoln and Socrates than Patton and Caesar.
- Good succession planning is a telling trait of great leaders; it shows they put the organization's success above their own.
- "Military" style leadership, with frequent criticism and infrequent praise, is often used but rarely effective. Even the military has moved away from it.

Further Reading

Good to Great, by Jim Collins, Harper Business, 2001. A business classic, and for good reason. Analyzes the common characteristics of companies that have sustained, great performance.

Primal Leadership, by Daniel Goleman, Harvard Business Press, 2002. Goleman popularized the phrase "emotional intelligence" and helps businesspeople understand what it takes to truly motivate others.

Leadership, by James MacGregor Burns, HarperCollins, 1978. This is the classic text on leadership and is still worth reading.

Firing Back: How Great Leaders Rebound after Career Disasters, by Jeffrey Sonnenfeld and Andrew Ward, Harvard Business Press, 2007. A look at how some prominent business leaders have bounced back from career-shattering episodes.

If I go back to when the debt markets froze up and you had the collapse of Lehman Brothers, there was a lot of panic. . . .

Napoleon said the role of a leader is to define reality and give hope. In a crisis, you've got to define reality, you've got to set a context. But then what you can't say is look, the building is on fire, but I have no way of getting out. What you've got to say is: Here are the pathways out. We may have to go floor by floor, but you want to communicate to people the progress you are making, and they will have confidence in you, if you were realistic about the portrayal of the crisis and the consequences.

KENNETH CHENAULT, *CEO, American Express, in a video interview for* The Wall Street Journal's *Lessons in Leadership series*

Chapter **THREE**

MOTIVATION

To be a great leader, you must understand your followers. What motivates them? What do they want? What do they fear? What makes them tick? How do you get them to give their very best efforts to the cause?

It starts with the most fundamental question in management studies: Why do people work? How you answer that question tells volumes about your management style.

A century ago, Frederick Winslow Taylor answered the question in the simplest terms: people want high wages. They work because they have to, to make the money, to survive. If they didn't have to work, they wouldn't.

But do people really work because they have to? Do they work primarily to make money, or to meet their basic needs? We all know people who pour themselves into work that they don't have to do. We're all familiar with the volunteer who works harder than the paid staff, or the "dollar-a-year" executive who seldom goes home to sleep. For most of us, even a modest degree of self-examination reveals that "because we have to" or "for the money" are, at best, only partial answers to the very complex question of why we work.

Douglas McGregor explored this topic in his breakthrough 1960 book, *The Human Side of Enterprise*. McGregor was a founding faculty member of MIT's Sloan School of Management, named after Alfred P. Sloan, who ran General Motors in the 1920s and 1930s. Sloan was in many ways the successor of Frederick Winslow Taylor's scientific school of management. But ironically, McGregor's work was dedicated to debunking the very sort of command-and-control management that Sloan and Taylor had championed.

Behind the decisions and actions of every manager, McGregor argued, are a series of basic assumptions about human behavior. Most managers of the time seemed to subscribe to Theory X, with assumptions including:

- The average human being has an inherent dislike of work and will avoid it if he can.
- Because of this human characteristic of dislike of work, most people must be coerced, controlled, directed, threatened with punishment, to get them to put forth adequate effort toward the achievement of organizational objectives.
- The average human being prefers to be directed, wishes to avoid responsibility, has relatively little ambition, wants security above all.

As an alternative, McGregor offered up Theory Y, which rests on these assumptions:

- The expenditure of physical and mental effort in work is as natural as play or rest.
- External control and threat of punishment are not the only means for bringing about effort toward organizational objectives. Man will exercise self-direction and self-control in the service of objectives to which he is committed.

- Commitment to objectives is a function of the rewards associated with their achievement.

- The average human being learns, under proper conditions, not only to accept but to seek responsibility.

- The capacity to exercise a relatively high degree of imagination, ingenuity, and creativity in the solution of organizational problems is widely, not narrowly, distributed in the population.

- Under the conditions of modern industrial life, the intellectual potentialities of the average human being are only partly utilized.

In those six assumptions lie the roots of modern management. The goal, post-McGregor, is no longer simply to direct and control employees who, left to their own devices, will shun work. The goal is to create conditions that make them want to offer maximum effort on their own. Employees who harness self-direction and self-control in pursuit of common objectives, it turns out, are far more productive and effective than those working under a system of controls designed to force them to meet objectives they don't understand or share. If you give people responsibility, they often rise to the challenge. Unleashing the imagination and ingenuity and creativity of your employers can multiply their contributions many times over.

Simple stuff. But powerful consequences. In the half century since McGregor's book, the world has enjoyed an unprecedented era of innovation and prosperity built in no small part on organizational systems that harness the self-motivation of workers. McGregor's insights are at the foundation of a management revolution that has literally changed the way the world works.

But the irony—the tragedy, really—is that more than fifty years after McGregor's book was published, it's still easy to find managers who rely on Theory X assumptions—who believe fear and control are more effective tools of management than enthusiasm and responsibility. That's a testament to how slowly and poorly management knowledge makes its way into the workplace—what Pfeffer and Sutton have called the "Knowing-Doing" gap. We may know what's right, but we don't necessarily do it.

Just as troublesome as managers who still subscribe to Theory X, are those who misapply Theory Y. *The Office*'s Michael Scott is modern enough to know, as he occasionally professes, that it's all about "the people." He attempts to create a "soft" environment where praise is plentiful and boosting morale is the order of the day. But his is also an environment where any sense of commitment to ambitious goals is lost, and where mediocrity is coddled.

The misapplication of McGregor's "Theory Y" ideas leads to dead ends like the one captured in this dialogue from a *Dilbert* cartoon:

> WALLY: I find it rather demotivating that you never praise me for a job well done.
> POINTY-HEADED BOSS: You've never done a job well.
> WALLY: That's because I'm demotivated.
> POINTY-HEADED BOSS: You have to go first.
> WALLY: Wouldn't that make me the leader?

As this book will show, good management requires both a respect for individuals and their capacities, and an insistence on candor, accountability, and excellence. At the end of the day, Theory Y and Theory X aren't really mutually exclusive. Most people can and will exercise self-direction but also need some degree of guidance and oversight. Great leaders know how to encourage individual responsibility and initiative, but at the same time also make effective use of measurement and controls.

This may sound contradictory, but it's not. The greatest mistakes in management are made by those who go to one extreme or the other. A leader who relies entirely on strict rules, constant oversight, and intricate measurement systems to ride herd on employees will likely find those employees are dispirited and demotivated and, ultimately, won't give their best. But a leader who lavishes praise and leaves workers to their own devices, who doesn't clearly distinguish between high-performing employees and low-performing ones, will soon find performance suffering.

Successful managers, say Thomas Peters and Robert Waterman in *In Search of Excellence*, have a curious blend of X and Y. It's what they call the "simultaneous loose-tight properties" of great organizations:

> Messrs. Watson (IBM), Kroc (McDonald's), Marriott, et al., have been pathbreakers in treating people as adults, in inducing practical innovation and contributions from tens of thousands, in providing training and development opportunities for all, in treating all as members of the family. Mr. Watson, in fact, in carrying out his open door policy had an unfailing weakness for the worker; his managers rarely won when a worker complaint was surfaced.
>
> On the other hand, all of these gentlemen were tough as nails. All were ruthless when their core values of service to the customer and unstinting quality were violated. They combined, then, a caring side and a tough side. Like good parents, they cared a lot—and expected a lot. To oversimplify their characteristics as predominantly "X-ish" or "Y-ish" is almost entirely to miss the point.

But enough for the theory. Let's get down to the specifics of just how you motivate your people.

DOES PAY MATTER?

Of course it does. People expect to be paid for their work.

But how important is pay to achieving organizational greatness? It turns out, not as important as you might think.

Numerous studies have attempted to find a clear link between pay practices and performance but have largely failed. In *Good to Great*, Jim Collins said his team "found no systematic pattern linking executive compensation to the process of going from good to great." There was no indication, for instance, that bonuses or stock options were more widely used by the good-to-great companies. Moreover, Collins found that the executives who led the good-to-great transition actually received slightly less total cash compensation than their counterparts at comparison companies.

Pfeffer and Sutton come to a similar conclusion about most efforts to boost performance by creating pay incentives:

> There is, in fact, little evidence that equity incentives of any kind, including stock options, enhance organizational performance. One review of more than 220 studies concluded that equity ownership had no consistent effect on financial performance. Another massive study and review of research on executive compensation published by the National Bureau of Economic Research reported that most schemes designed to align managerial and shareholder interests failed to do so.

It's not that people don't respond to financial incentives. They clearly do. When you pay salespeople commissions based on their sales, for instance, they will always sell more than when you simply pay them a flat salary. The same goes for an individual crafts person, who gets paid on a per-piece basis.

The *Journal*'s Jon Auerbach captured the kind of supercharged environment that pay incentives can create in a profile of a salesman for EMC Corporation named John Chatwin in 1998. At the time, the company paid salespeople about 65 percent of their total pay in commissions and put no cap on the commissions they could earn.

The story begins with Chatwin, an ex-college hockey player, fearing he won't make his sales target for the quarter. To ensure that doesn't happen, he shifts into overdrive, calling clients while ferrying relatives to his son's christening, and breaking away from a family barbecue to contact a customer about a deal. "I may not be brilliant," Chatwin told Auerbach, "but I'm hungry, I'm scrappy."

The problem, however, is that most jobs today aren't like Chatwin's, where performance depends largely on individual effort and can be easily measured. Today's jobs generally involve teamwork. Success is less due to an individual's effort, and measurement of individual effort becomes more complex, if not impossible. In these situations, pay for performance can often seem unfair and arbitrary, and the result can demotivate, rather than motivate, employees. Resentment can fester, and significant time and energy can be wasted by people trying to get personal credit rather than working for team success.

The bottom line is this: incentive pay is an effective tool in situations where performance can be fairly measured and where it is based largely on individual effort. But it is less effective in situations—common in today's workplace—where the measurements are highly subjective and the work is done by teams.

COMMITMENT TO GOALS

If pay isn't the key to encouraging great performance and attracting and keeping great people, what is?

A half-century ago, social scientist Abraham Maslow outlined a pyramid that showed what he called the human being's "hierarchy of needs."

People start with a desire for basic physiological needs: food, clothing, shelter—that's the bottom of the pyramid. Once they've achieved those, they seek safety, and then social interaction and love, and then self-esteem. Finally, at the top of the pyramid, is what Maslow called "self actualization"—the need to fulfill one's self and become all that one is capable of being.

Today, most workers—and particularly the best workers—have made their way to the top of Maslow's pyramid. Basic needs are taken care of. They want something more.

"Making a living is no longer enough," writes Drucker. "Work also has to make a life." If you want to keep good people, work needs to provide them with a sense they are doing something important, that they are fulfilling their destiny. And at the end of the day, these psychological needs are likely to be as important, perhaps more important, than the salary you pay.

In other words, work must give meaning. As a manager, you are the maker of meanings. You need to make sure your team is personally committed to the goals of the organization, that they feel those goals are worth achieving, and that they feel they are playing a significant role in achieving those goals.

That's a complex challenge, not easily summed up in a few simple rules or guidelines. One of the best descriptions I've found of the complex social and psychological elements that go into creating a satisfying workplace is in Tracy Kidder's Pulitzer Prize–winning book, *The Soul of a New Machine*. Kidder skillfully recorded the human drama, and, ultimately, the magic that motivated a team of engineers at Data General in the 1970s to develop a new generation of computer.

The Data General team worked with little formal encouragement from the company's top management. But they came to believe in what they were doing. At the end of his book, Kidder compares the people on the team to the stonemasons who built the great cathedrals.

> They were building temples to God. It was the sort of work that gave meaning to life. That's what [team leader Tom] West and his team of engineers were looking for, I think. They themselves liked to say they didn't work on their machine for money. In the aftermath, some of them felt that they were receiving neither the loot nor the recognition they had earned, and some said they were a little bitter on that score. But when they talked about the project itself, their enthusiasm returned. It lit up their faces. Many seemed to want to say that they had participated in something quite out of the ordinary.

That's the magic of managing talented people—making them feel they are participating in something valuable, something unique, something out of the ordinary. The manager's job is to get his team to make a commitment—to one another, to the goals of the group, to a cause that is greater than themselves. That commitment, it turns out, is worth more than gold.

MOTIVATION in Brief

- Work is as natural as play or rest. Under the right circumstances, most people will exercise self-direction and self-control in pursuit of common objectives.
- Ordinary people will make extraordinary efforts to achieve goals to which they are committed. The key is to get them committed.
- There is mixed evidence as to whether pay incentives improve performance in most circumstances.

Further Reading

The Human Side of Enterprise, by Douglas McGregor, 1960. Republished by McGraw-Hill, 2006. This is clearly one of the most important management books ever written, and it revolutionized thinking about management of people. McGregor's "Theory Y" held that individuals are self-motivated and self-directed and don't need to be coerced into work.

Maslow on Management, by Abraham Maslow. Initially published in the 1960s under the impenetrable name *Eupsychian Management,* republished by John Wiley and Sons, 1998. This book is a struggle to read but it applies the pathbreaking ideas of Maslow's "hierarchy of needs" to the practice of management.

The Soul of a New Machine, by Tracy Kidder, Little, Brown and Company, 1981. This book is a joy to read, and more than any other, brings to life the complex reasons why people find satisfaction in their work.

THE
WALL
STREET
JOURNAL.

One of the main things I always look for [in hiring] is the personality—how that person interacts with you during the interview, how you think they are going to fit in. You want to build a team of people who want to work with each other, who get excited to work with each other, who want to get up every day and tackle some of these tough problems.

Now that we're part of Google, it's more of an algorithm. . . .

CHAD HURLEY, *CEO, YouTube,*
in a video interview for The Wall Street Journal's
Lessons in Leadership series

Chapter FOUR

PEOPLE

With the possible exception of Peter Drucker, no single person has had a greater impact on the practice of management in modern times than John F. Welch Jr.—universally known as "Jack."

Welch spent forty-one years at the General Electric Company— half of them as chairman and chief executive—and during that time he transformed the giant institution. Like many large companies of the time, GE had become heavy with corporate bureaucracy and planning. Welch hated bureaucracy, was infamously impatient, and scolded managers who presented him with lengthy memos and fat documents. "I don't want planning," he'd lecture them. "I want plans."

Statistics tell the story: he slashed the company's bloated middle management ranks by eliminating more than 100,000 jobs—a quarter of the company's workforce. And he presided over a massive wave of acquisitions, buying 993 companies with a total value of just over $130 billion. By the turn of the century, he was running not just one of the largest, but one of the most admired, companies in the world.

Critics try to diminish Welch's accomplishments by pointing out that the 1980s and 1990s were a period of surging economic growth, and he was simply steering a giant ship on top of that unstoppable wave. But one has only to look at what happened to GE's rival from the

1950s and 1960s, Westinghouse Electric Company, during the same period to realize how significant Welch's accomplishment was. Westinghouse has now all but disappeared, while GE remains one of the most fabled companies in the world.

In his early years, Welch's rabid cost cutting earned him the name "Neutron Jack" and the enmity of labor union leaders everywhere. But in his later years, Welch became known for the attention he devoted to developing his people. He recognized that it was his stable of managers who, at the end of the day, were responsible for making GE shine. He put the human resources function at the center of GE culture and spent countless hours at the company's Crotonville, N.Y., training center, talking with rising managers. He claimed to spend "at least 50 percent of my time" working on "people issues." In the end, the greatest testimony to his impact on business culture is the fact that so many of his alumni went on to run other giant corporations, in the United States and abroad—companies such as Boeing, Pfizer, Home Depot, Fannie Mae, and ABB. GE has arguably trained more top executives than any of the nation's business schools.

In Welch's view, his image as the hard-charging, job-slashing enemy of bureaucracy and his image as the champion of the middle manager were not in any way at odds. In an interview with my colleagues Carol Hymowitz and Matt Murray shortly before he stepped down as CEO, Welch told the story of an early job at GE where he experienced the frustration of working for a boss who tried to encourage group unity by instituting a "level" rewards system.

At the end of the year, we all got the exact same $1,000 raise. I said, "This isn't for me, I have to get out of here." But my boss asked me to stay, and I never had that problem again.

That experience made me aware of what the frustrations can be for others in a large company like GE. You drive into the big parking lot, put your car among rows and rows of other cars, go into the office, and some horse's ass tells you what to do and how to do it. And this isn't what you expected out of life. If you don't get recognized and you have the wrong boss, it can be awful.

Welch said he advised employees to "never allow themselves to become victims in an institution."

I encourage them to raise their hands, to be seen, to make a statement. I tell them, "If GE can't be the place where you can get rid of that victim feeling, go somewhere else." And we try to weed out the managers who make employees feel like victims, the managers who lose staff all the time.

Today, many of Welch's hard-edged personnel practices are criticized in business schools and elsewhere, for demoralizing employees and undercutting team spirit. We'll air those debates in the chapter that follows. But given the extraordinary successes the Welch way has racked up over the years, we're inclined to give him the benefit of the doubt.

HIRING AND FIRING

Choosing people may be the most important responsibility any manager faces. In the research for his book *Good to Great*, Jim Collins found that high-performing CEOs focused first on getting "the right people on the bus and the wrong people off the bus" before figuring out where to drive it. They put people before strategy. Best to start with a group of people committed to working together, then let them figure out the vision.

"Great vision without great people," Collins concluded, "is irrelevant."

Welch certainly shares that view. In his book *Winning*, he says he starts the hiring process with three acid tests: for *integrity*, *intelligence*, and *maturity*. "People with integrity tell the truth and they keep their word," he writes. "They take responsibility for past actions, admit mistakes, and fix them." On intelligence, Welch makes clear he's not necessarily looking for education, but rather "a strong dose of intellectual curiosity, with a breadth of knowledge to work with or lead other smart people in today's complex world." As for maturity, Welch says it has nothing to do with age; rather it's a sense that the person "can withstand the heat, handle stress and setbacks, and alternatively, when those wonderful moments arrive, enjoy success with equal parts of joy and humility."

Only if candidates pass those three acid tests does he then begin to evaluate what he calls "the four Es." They are:

- **Positive energy.** Does the candidate have the ability to thrive on action and relish change? Will he or she be able to start the day with enthusiasm, and end it that way, too? "People with positive energy," writes Welch, who clearly has plenty of his own, "just love life."
- **The ability to energize others.** "People who energize can inspire their teams to take on the impossible," he writes. That requires the right combination of knowledge and skills of persuasion.
- **Edge,** which Welch defines as the ability to make tough yes-or-no decisions. "Anyone can look at an issue from every different angle," he writes. "Some smart people can—and will—analyze those angles indefinitely. But effective people

know when to stop assessing and make a tough call, even without total information."

- **Execute,** or the ability to get the job done. Welch says experience has taught him that some people can do well on the first three Es but still not have what is needed to take a job over the finish line. He looks to hire people who can make things happen.

Finally, Welch evaluates his candidates for their "passion." "By passion," he writes, "I mean a heartfelt, deep, and authentic excitement about work."

FIRING

While hiring may be one of the most important jobs of the manager, firing is surely one of the most unpleasant. It is never easy. But the key to making this event go relatively smoothly is not what you say or do in the final meeting; rather it's what you have said and done in the months leading up to it.

As discussed above, the best workplaces are built on clear expectations and candid feedback. In such a workplace, firing may be unpleasant, but it won't be a shock. And often, poor-performing workers will read the writing on the wall and leave or find another job before a firing becomes necessary.

Welch calls this the first rule of firing: no surprises. "In the ideal situation," he writes, "the last conversation will go like this:"

Boss: Well, I think you know what this meeting is about.
Employee: Yes, I guess I do. So what are your thoughts on timing, and what's the deal?

Welch's second rule of firing, also a good one, is this: minimize humiliation.

Even after firing an employee, the manager remains responsible for helping him or her through the next step. "Build up his confidence," writes Welch. "Coach him. Let him know there is a good job for him out there, where his skills are a better match. You may even help him find that job. Your goal for the fired employee is a soft landing, wherever he goes."

RANK AND YANK

This is one of the hottest debates in management. Welch was famous for forcing his managers to rank all employees on a 1-to-5 scale, giving about 10 percent of them a 1 and at least 10 percent a 5. The "1s" and a roughly equal number of "2s" were showered with praise, affection, and generous financial rewards. The middle 70 percent—the "3s" and "4s"— were given coaching, training, and thoughtful goal setting, with an eye toward giving them an opportunity to move into the top. And the "5s" were expected to leave GE.

"There is no sugarcoating this," Welch says. "They have to go."

Critics say this forced ranking undermines teamwork. It encourages employees to engage in destructive and wasteful game playing designed to ensure they get credit, or others don't.

Pfeffer and Sutton are among the most fervent critics. They cited a survey of more than 200 human resources professionals from companies employing more than 2,500 people that found that in more than half of the companies that used forced ranking, respondents "reported that forced ranking resulted in lower productivity, inequity, and skepticism, negative effects on employee engagement, reduced collaboration, and damage to morale and mistrust in leadership."

Still, there's plenty of evidence to suggest that to have a high-performance workplace, you need to be constantly identifying and rewarding your top performers, and continuously culling low performers.

It's too easy to fall into a "squeaky wheel" pattern, where financial rewards go to those employees who make the most noise, or who regularly drum up outside job offers. That's a mistake. If you identify your top performers and reward them up front, before the competition comes calling, you'll be much better off.

Likewise, getting rid of poor performers, while unpleasant, is critical to maintaining a culture of excellence. In the end, success at maintaining a high-performing culture requires the use of both carrots and sticks.

"You have to go along with a can of fertilizer in one hand and water in the other and constantly throw both on the flowers," Welch said in the *Journal* interview shortly before he stepped down. "If they grow, you have a beautiful garden. If they don't, you cut them out. That's what management is all about."

SHOULD YOU DO PERFORMANCE EVALUATIONS?

This is another hotly debated topic in management circles.

Proponents say candid and honest assessment of an employee's performance is absolutely critical to a smoothly functioning workplace. People have a right to know what's expected of them; and they certainly have a right to know if they are failing to live up to expectations. Performance reviews provide that.

But opponents say performance reviews unnecessarily undermine morale and reinforce a command-and-control structure. In an article published in *The Wall Street Journal*, UCLA management professor Samuel Culbert launched an all-out attack on the practice.

"To my way of thinking," Culbert wrote, "a one-side accountable, boss-administered review is little more than a dysfunctional pretense.

It's negative to corporate performance, an obstacle to straight-talk relationships, and a prime cause of low morale at work. Even the mere knowledge that such an event will take place damages daily communications and teamwork."

At the heart of the issue is a little problem of self-deceit. Like the children of Garrison Keillor's Lake Wobegon, most workers think of themselves as above average. And it's not entirely clear what purpose is served by telling half of them they aren't.

"We all think we're tops," write Peters and Waterman. "We're exuberantly, wildly irrational about ourselves. And that has sweeping implications for organizing." Our exuberance helps us achieve ambitious goals. Puncturing that exuberance makes success less likely.

Like so many other issues addressed in this book, the answer isn't a simple yes or no. At most workplaces, performance reviews can be both a valuable and even necessary tool. In the successful workplace, employees must get clear performance feedback. Mediocrity cannot and should not be tolerated. It undermines the morale of those who are doing their best. And employees should always have a firm sense of where they stand in the organization. A performance-related firing, for instance, should never come as a surprise to the fired worker. If it does, management has failed.

But systems of appraising performance work best if they are based on a dialogue between the manager and the employee; if they emphasize successes and not failures; if they criticize bad behaviors without undercutting the value of the employee; and if any negative feedback occurs as soon as possible after the behavior that's being criticized. Moreover, the appraisal process needs to acknowledge the fact that the manager shares in responsibility for the worker's success. Performance reviews need to be a two-way conversation.

Moreover, the bulk of the review should not look back, but rather look forward. It shouldn't be primarily a critique of what the employee has done in the past, but rather an opportunity to set goals and expectations for the period ahead. Used in this way, performance reviews can become a critical tool for motivation.

EMPLOYEE ENGAGEMENT

Motivating knowledge workers to do their best for the organization ultimately comes down to making work meaningful. That may be the manager's most important and yet most challenging task. It's easier said than done.

In recent decades, the Gallup organization has surveyed workers at various U.S. companies in an effort to determine whether they are actively engaged. The surveys show that in the average organization, there is only one actively engaged employee for every five who are disengaged. But in high-performing companies, the ratio is reversed—as many as eight engaged employees for every disengaged employee.

A study by the Institute for Employment Studies concluded that the engaged worker:

- Believes in the organization he or she works for;
- Works to make things at the organization better;
- Has some understanding of the business context, or "big picture," that the organization operates in;
- Respects and helps colleagues in the organization;
- Is willing to go the "extra mile" on the job;
- Works to keep up to date with developments in the field.

The payoff of having an engaged workforce is huge. But how do you make workers feel engaged? This is similar to the challenge Welch identifies in avoiding workers who feel like nameless "victims." Countless books have been written on this topic in recent years. But in the end, their major advice boils down to a few broad themes:

- Workers must feel they are involved in the decision making;
- They must feel their work is important;
- They must feel they can voice their views and be listened to by management;
- They must feel they have opportunities to develop in their jobs;
- They must believe that the organization is doing important, meaningful work;
- They must believe the organization is at some level concerned with their health and well-being;
- They must feel their engagement is appreciated and rewarded.

There is a tendency in some organizations for employee engagement to be treated as the concern of the "HR Shop." But to be effective, it has to be central to the job of every manager. If your employees don't feel engaged, you are doing something wrong.

Of course, like all good management ideas, this one is subject to abuse and misuse. Indeed, the importance of "employee engagement" as a management concept was in some ways confirmed when the *Dilbert* comic strip satirized it in November 2009.

POINTY-HEADED BOSS: We need more of what the management experts call "Employee Engagement." I don't know the details, but it has something to do with you idiots working harder for the same pay.

DILBERT: Is anything different on your end?

POINTY-HEADED BOSS: I think I'm supposed to be happier.

MANAGING DIFFICULT PEOPLE

One of the most common complaints of new managers goes something like this:

> I've waited years to get this job. I wanted to be a manager so I could use my skills to build something important—to develop new products, to find new markets, to grow an organization. Instead, I feel like I'm spending most of my time dealing with people problems.
>
> These people are all well-educated, well-paid professionals. So why do I suddenly feel like a kindergarten teacher?

Sound familiar? Well sorry, folks, but it comes with the territory. At the end of the day, management *is* about people. And the fact that you spend most of your time dealing with people problems simply means you are doing your job. It would be nice if all your employees were high-performance and low-maintenance, and did their jobs with a minimum of unnecessary angst and drama. But life doesn't work like that.

Still, it's frustrating. And here's the most frustrating part: there's a good chance the most difficult people will be among your most valuable and talented people.

Life would be easier if that weren't the case. If an average or marginal employee misbehaves—throws tantrums in public, yells abusively at teammates, routinely skips important meetings, refuses to share critical information—you know what to do. You call the employee in, you candidly lay out the damaging behavior, you tell him (or her) to clean up his act, and you either implicitly or explicitly make it clear that if the behavior continues, there will be consequences.

But what if the person misbehaving is your star employee? You know the type: someone who works endless hours and is driven to succeed, but who then demands inordinate praise and reinforcement for their successes. Someone who feels it necessary to exceed every expectation you have for them, in part because (pardon a little armchair psychology here) they could never satisfy the high expectations of a parent or some other authority figure in their past, and at their core feel some unaccountable lack of self-esteem.

Such a person might feel compelled to dominate meetings to show off their brilliance, and thus intimidate other participants. Or they may berate others in the office who don't meet their high standards of hard work and achievement. Or they may simply demand your attention and praise at every turn, undercutting your ability to do your job and effectively lead other members of the team.

In this book, we advocate candor as an indispensable tool for most management challenges. But with the talented but troubled employee described above, candor can be disastrous. Even a modest effort to point out bad behavior can lead to a major blowup. Your star employee may suddenly decide he or she is unappreciated and move to one of the other jobs that is always waiting.

What should you do in such a case?

First of all, recognize that, as strange as it may seem to you, your A player's misbehavior likely arises from insecurity. Even though you may think he or she already gets an inordinate amount of praise and reinforcement, give more. You may resent having to spend the extra time providing reassurance to someone who, in your view, doesn't need it, but do it anyway.

Then, after you've demonstrated your willingness to go the extra mile—or extra ten miles—or extra hundred miles, if necessary—attempt to have a gentle conversation about the behavior you're finding unhelpful. Be sure to do this in private. If you do it in the presence of coworkers, you'll only feed his or her insecurities. And avoid suggestions of blame; rather, try to enlist the person's help in solving the workplace problem.

Beyond that, look for creative structural solutions. If the problem is that a person is dominating meetings, try to find a way to ensure they attend fewer meetings—perhaps by "promoting" them to a job in which you ask them to advise you directly on problems, which "frees" them from attending a lot of unnecessary and time-consuming meetings. If they are abusing coworkers in a work space, give them a private office as a reward for their hard work.

Finally, if all else fails, be willing to let them go. Very few employees are truly indispensable. And the pervasive damage that a badly behaving player can cause to the rest of your team is hard to overstate.

MANAGING BURNT-OUT EMPLOYEES

In most organizations, you're likely to find a core of midcareer people, usually between the ages of thirty-five and fifty-five, who have hit a wall. They are often long-serving, loyal, and committed, but over time they may have grown frustrated, bored, and perhaps frightened by a sneaking suspicion that their careers have peaked.

You could toss them all out and replace them with younger workers—but that would be begging for an age discrimination lawsuit. Moreover, you'd be losing some very valuable institutional knowledge and experience in the process.

Our advice instead is to devote some serious time and energy to reenergizing your midcareer employees, and getting them committed anew to their work. As mentioned above, it's keeping that commitment that's critical to your success.

For starters, make it a point to talk with midcareer employees. Ask them about their career hopes and aspirations, and ask them what they would like to be doing five or ten years hence. Odds are their ambition hasn't died, it's just gone into hibernation. A bit of high-level attention could bring it out once again.

Once you've learned more about their aspirations, look for new assignments you can give them that play into their life plans. You'd be surprised how even the most listless of employees can spring to life when given a new, meaningful challenge.

You might also consider putting some of these players into mentoring roles for younger workers. This has multiple benefits for the organization: it makes older workers feel valued for their experience, it gives them a chance to benefit from the energy and engagement of younger workers, and it gives younger workers a chance to benefit from the experience of older workers.

Finally, leadership development programs, training programs, and just straight sabbaticals can all help middle-aged workers gain a fresh commitment to their jobs. Some combination is certainly worth trying.

MANAGING FOR DIVERSITY

It has become accepted wisdom in the business world that a diverse workforce—reflecting both ethnic and gender diversity—makes for a stronger organization. Most of the large corporations based in the United States and Europe have instituted high-level programs to encourage diversity.

There are three reasons usually given as to why diversity makes organizations stronger:

- A diverse workforce brings a diversity of viewpoints and backgrounds to the table, and results in better and more innovative decisions;
- A diverse workforce is better able to serve a diverse customer base;
- A diverse workforce is better able to attract and retain talent from a diverse population.

While all three arguments have strong appeal, the formal evidence that diversity improves business performance remains mixed. In some organizations, diversity programs have clearly increased innovation, improved customer service, and boosted talent recruitment and retention. In others, however, diversity programs can impose a cost—forcing managers to spend too much time and energy focusing on recruiting and retaining people who fit certain ethnic categories rather than finding the best people for the job.

We strongly recommend that you make diversity a central tenet of your approach to hiring and building your team, for one simple reason: unless you do so, you are likely to fall prey to the human tendency to surround yourself with others like yourself. That could cause you to run afoul of federal laws prohibiting discrimination on the basis of race, color, religion, sex, or national origin. More important, it's also likely to deprive you of the best people to do the job.

That doesn't mean you should set aside certain jobs for, say, blacks or Latinos or women (or, for that matter, white men). And it certainly doesn't mean you should hire unqualified job applicants for diversity's sake.

But it does mean that when you are recruiting for any position, you should make special efforts to reach out to diverse communities. You might advertise in minority publications, for instance, or use diverse recruiters. It's a good idea always to make sure that at least one of your final three job candidates for any job comes from a diverse background. If you don't have at least one qualified candidate from a diverse background, then you may want to extend your search for applicants.

Take the same approach when the time comes for making promotions. Make sure that you consider at least three candidates for any promotion, and that at least one of them is a diversity candidate. This discipline will help ensure that diversity remains a central part of your management thinking.

Finally, look for ways to stay in touch with your employees from diverse backgrounds. They may feel less comfortable talking with you than those who share your background. Find people in your group who can be their mentors. And look for ways to get honest feedback. You may need to create special training or development opportunities for those who haven't had the same professional opportunities that the majority of your group has had.

MANAGING WOMEN

We began this chapter with something of a paean to Jack Welch. But this is one important issue on which we think Welch has it wrong. (Even the wisest person can't be right all the time!)

Speaking at the Society of Human Resource Management's annual conference in June 2009, Welch created a stir by declaring "there's no such thing as work-life balance." Instead, he said, "There are work-life choices, and you make them, and they have consequences." If you take time off to raise children, and you miss a key promotion as a result, well, too bad.

When Welch's remarks were reported in WSJ.com, the comments came in fast and furious. "Well, pardon the heck out of me, but who asked him?" commented one. "Perhaps Jack Welch is on his third marriage because he's a chauvinist," said another.

Emotions aside, the facts here are pretty clear. In the United States these days, some 58 percent of college graduates are women, and nearly half of all professional and graduate degrees are earned by women. Yet somewhere along the way, women keep falling off the career ladder. They are woefully underrepresented in the ranks of top management, as well as in many lucrative careers like consulting, banking, and engineering.

We'll leave it to others to debate whether this reflects massive discrimination. But what it clearly does reflect is a massively underused resource. There are a lot of very talented women out there who aren't fully engaged in the workforce. And figuring out how to get them engaged can be a big boon for any manager.

So our advice to managers is this: pay some special attention to the women in your workforce. Figure out what you need to do to attract them, keep them, and advance them. Give people opportunities to take time off to raise their kids or care for an aging parent. It will pay off for your organization in the end.

In that regard, a few suggestions:

- Create off-ramps and on-ramps. Women are much more likely than men to seek periods of time away from work, often to deal with children or aging parents. Look for ways to facilitate those needs. Create reduced-hour jobs, create work-sharing arrangements, provide flexible work hours during the day, and explore work opportunities at home.
- Reduce the stigma attached to these special arrangements. There's no reason an at-home worker, or a reduced-hours worker, should be assumed to be less valuable to the organization than an on-the-job-all-day worker. It's up to you as a manager to make it clear that you support these kinds of arrangements.
- Hire women who've taken time off. It's difficult to get back into the workforce after being out of it for a while. But if you make a special effort to reach out to people who've done so, you may find some unrecognized gems.
- Finally, but perhaps most important, avoid creating a "male" culture in the workplace. Sorry to stereotype, but there are a whole set of workplace behaviors that are commonly recognized as being more common among women than men.

Women tend to seem less confident when expressing their views in large meetings. They are more likely to emphasize group unity over individual accomplishment. They are less aggressive about asking for promotions and raises.

As a manager, you need to be aware of these tendencies and try to correct for them. Don't let good ideas be overlooked because they are expressed in a tentative way. Don't ignore the individual accomplishments of people less likely to trumpet them. Don't give raises and promotions to the people who ask for them most often; give them to the people who deserve them most.

PEOPLE in Brief

- Great managers get the right people on the bus, and the wrong people off, before figuring out where to drive it.
- Employees need clear and candid performance feedback, so they know where they stand.
- Great organizations have more engaged employees than disengaged employees.
- A performance-related firing should never come as a surprise.
- In today's workforce, women are an underused resource. Figure out how to use them better.

Further Reading

Winning, by Jack Welch, with Suzy Welch, Collins, 2005. Welch's blunt-spoken style comes through in this book, written with his third wife. These are the ideas that earned Welch the title "Manager of the Century" from *Fortune* magazine.

Jack: Straight from the Gut, by Jack Welch with John A. Byrne, Warner Business Books, 2001. If you want to dive deeper into the cult of Jack, this autobiography is a fascinating read.

Harvard Business Review on Talent Management, Harvard Business Press, 2008. An excellent series of articles on key challenges of talent management, from keeping "A" players productive to managing "middlescence."

In many companies, strategy plans are very secretive, only known by the executive board, and then they are discussing why the employees are not following. Well, why should they, when they don't even know what the plan is? You must have the courage to put it out in public and be ready to defend it.

I think there are similarities between the public life of a politician and life of a CEO. You need to understand that they have to reelect you as a leader.

DITLEV ENGEL, *CEO, Vestas Wind Systems,*
in a video interview for The Wall Street Journal's
Lessons in Leadership series

Chapter **FIVE**

STRATEGY

You're ready to lead, but where are you going?

Charting a course—that's a fundamental responsibility of the manager. What is the *mission* of the organization you are managing? What is the *strategy* for accomplishing that mission? What are your *goals* for the future, and are they consistent with the strategy and mission? What are the overall goals for your team, and the individual goals for each member of the team?

It's remarkable how many managers never answer these basic questions. Sometimes they may take their mission, strategy, and goals as givens—determined by their boss, or their boss's boss, or perhaps just determined by the nature of the organization they work within. Many managers will spend their entire work lives reacting—reacting to orders from above, reacting to pressures and problems from below, or simply reacting to the insistent demands of a busy workplace, but never setting a clear direction of their own.

If all you do is *react*, you will fail. You may be good at solving problems that arise. You may be skilled at responding to the needs and requests of those you work for, or the people on your team. You may work long hours, be loved and respected by your employees, and be the very model of organizational efficiency. But if you aren't setting a direction, then you aren't doing the job.

Managers must know where they are going and have a clear plan for getting there.

This sounds simple, but in practice it takes extraordinary discipline. To understand why, take a single day in your own life and analyze your actions. How much of what you do in a day is in conscious pursuit of goals you set for yourself? The unique gift of being human is self-awareness—the ability to think about, and ultimately make decisions about, what you do with your life. But it is a gift often forgotten or trampled in the hubbub of daily life as we respond to the demands of others, or react to external stimuli, or deal with unexpected crises, or simply fulfill biological needs—to eat, to sleep, to make it through the day.

For the manager, the problem is multiplied many times over. As a manager, you are responsible for a whole group of people who have their own needs and demands and expect you to help meet them. You have a number of tasks you are expected to perform each day, and a schedule of meetings you must attend. Odds are you'll deal daily with several people who at least act as if they are your boss, telling you what you need to be doing. And then there are the other colleagues, customers, contractors, suppliers—a vast web of people—who have their own ideas about how you should spend your time.

In such a work environment, it's easy to focus on the problems. You may have an overbearing boss, you may have an extremely limited budget, you may not have enough people to do the job you've been asked to do, you may be part of a culture that is hugely resistant to change. In thousands of ways, your actions may be constrained.

But to be a good manager, you cannot get bogged down in what you *can't* do. Your job as a manager is to focus on what you *can* and *should* do, and how to get it done.

Many popular management books deal with this fundamental challenge. In Stephen Covey's bestseller, *The 7 Habits of Highly Effective People,* habit number one is "be proactive." *Proactivity,* Covey writes, "is a word you won't find in most dictionaries. It means more than merely taking initiative. It means that as human beings, we are responsible for our own lives. Our behavior is a function of our decisions, not our conditions."

As a manager, your responsibility to be proactive expands to your whole team. Take charge. Don't be a prisoner of habit or tradition. Don't get trapped in some predecessor's long obsolete agenda. Don't let the demands of others keep you and your group from doing what you know you should be doing. Don't focus on the constraints. Focus on the possibilities. Being a manager means you have been called on to exercise that most fundamental and valuable gift of human existence: to choose. To set a course. To determine your destiny.

Covey's first rule, to "be proactive," is followed by an equally important second rule: "begin with the end in mind." You need to know where you want to go. You need a plan to get there. And then each decision along the way can be made with an eye toward fulfilling that plan and reaching the goal.

George W. Bush, the nation's first MBA president, once famously declared: "I am the decider"—his version of Harry Truman's famous saying, "The buck stops here." But while making decisions is a critical part of the manager's job, those decisions are worth little if they don't fit into some broader plan, and if they don't keep the organization on a path to some larger goals. That's the essence of strategic thinking: understanding how each small decision a manager makes helps lead to a desired destination.

Most organizations divide the process into three steps. First, there is the overall *mission* of the organization. In the simplest and clearest terms, what is it you are setting out to do? Then there is your *strategy*— what is a realistic plan for accomplishing your mission, given the environment in which you operate? And then finally, there is an intricate set of individual and operational *goals*, the things that each team member must accomplish, and the timetable for accomplishing them, consistent with strategy and mission.

These things aren't set in cement. Goals may be reset regularly, to take into account changes in the environment and changes in resources, or to take advantage of new opportunities. Strategy should be changed less frequently—strategies need time to be successful, and a constantly changing strategy can be disruptive to an organization. Mission should change least of all: as long as your employees have a clear sense of the end destination, they can accept changing goals and readjusting strategies along the way.

A word of caution: though defining mission, strategy, and goals is central to the manager's job, the effort to do so sometimes becomes an end in itself, and a source of distraction. Endless exercises and off-site meetings dedicated to writing mission statements, planning strategies, and defining goals can become disconnected from the realities of day-to-day management. And the results can be detrimental to the organization.

For a brief time in my career, I was employed by CNBC—then a unit of General Electric—as chief of the cable network's Washington bureau. At one point, I needed the help of the director of human resources in solving a particularly thorny problem. Yet each time I called her office, I was told she was in a "Six Sigma" meeting. She never called back.

Doesn't at least one of the Sigmas, I thought at the time, require you to do your job?

In the end, as we will discuss later in this chapter and in the next one, strategy is only valuable if it is intricately connected to the process of *execution*. A survey of management consultants in the 1980s concluded that only 10 percent of effectively formulated management strategies were successfully implemented. That's a frightfully low success rate. Mission, strategy, goals, they are the right places to start. But they are *only* a start.

THE MISSION STATEMENT

Every organization needs a mission statement.

In the last chapter, we talked about how managers are makers of meaning. The mission statement is the highest articulation of that meaning. It gives everyone in the organization a shared focus and a shared goal. It helps create unity of purpose.

One of history's most famous mission statements came from President John F. Kennedy, who in 1961 committed the nation to, "before the decade is out, landing a man on the moon and returning him safely to earth."

In the years since, some have found fault with this mission. The speech announcing the plan was filled with rhetoric about the challenges from the Soviet Union, which a few years earlier had successfully launched the *Sputnik* satellite. Yet it was never really clear that sending a man to the moon had much to do with winning the war against communism.

Moreover, sending a man into space, as opposed to, say, launching a variety of unmanned probes, was a task filled with expensive complexities. To understand and master the universe, was it really necessary or even particularly helpful for a man to travel through it?

Nevertheless, Kennedy's proclamation was bold, inspirational, simple, and clear. It captured the public imagination. It rallied a dispirited nation around an aspirational goal that, while certainly challenging, in the end proved achievable.

As a mission statement, it is hard to beat.

While mission statements vary greatly from organization to organization, they generally attempt to answer the following three questions:

- What do we do?
- How do we do it?
- For whom do we do it?

Consider, for instance, this mission statement from Chiron, a unit of the pharmaceutical company Novartis:

Protecting people through innovative science by:

- Working to cure cancer
- Providing safe blood
- Preventing infectious diseases

That's about as clear as it gets. It tells you exactly what the company aims to do—cure cancer, provide safe blood supplies, and develop vaccines and other tools for preventing infectious disease. It tells you how it goes about reaching those goals—through innovative science. And it clearly states that the company exists to serve its patients.

But then, is it really that simple? Does the company really exist solely for the patients? What about its shareholders? Or its employees? Health care companies frequently put patients at the center of their mission—Amgen Inc., for instance, has a three-word mission statement: "To serve patients." Yet the more skeptical among us may wonder whether that's the only goal.

In answering the "For whom do we do it?" question, many companies have chosen to provide multiple answers. Dollar General Corporation, for instance, divides its mission into three parts:

For Customers . . . A Better Life
For Shareholders . . . A Superior Return
For Employees . . . Respect and Opportunity

Johnson & Johnson has a famous credo that has hung on the walls of the company for more than sixty years, and delineates the company's responsibilities, first, to doctors, nurses and patients; second, to employees; third, to the communities "in which we live and work"; and fourth, to shareholders. Other mission statements may refer to partners, patrons, or clients. In the real world, most organizations have more than one group of people they are committed to serving, and the mission statement needs to recognize that.

The "How do we do it?" question also raises the question of values. Many companies will add a statement of values to the mission statement; others will incorporate those values into the mission statement itself. Amgen's three-word mission statement, for instance, is followed by a list of "our values" that does a more complete job of describing the company's goals:

- Be Science-Based
- Compete Intensely and Win
- Create Value for Patients, Staff, and Stockholders
- Be Ethical
- Trust and Respect Each Other
- Ensure Quality
- Work in Teams
- Collaborate, Communicate, and Be Accountable

Ben & Jerry's Homemade, Inc.—the ice cream company that's known for its commitment to social causes—has what seems to me to be one of the best-thought-out mission statements that accurately combines the company's multiple goals, values, and constituencies:

Our mission consists of three interrelated parts:
Product Mission: To make, distribute, and sell the finest

quality all natural ice cream and euphoric concoctions with a continued commitment to incorporating wholesome, natural ingredients, and promoting business practices that respect the Earth and Environment.

Economic Mission: To operate the company on a sustainable financial basis of profitable growth, increasing value for our stakeholders, and expanding opportunities for development and career growth for our employees.

Social Mission: To operate the company in a way that actively recognizes the central role that business plays in society by initiating innovative ways to improve the quality of life locally, nationally, and internationally.

How long should a mission statement be? In his book *101 Mission Statements from Top Companies*, Jeffrey Abrahams quotes Abraham Lincoln's response, when asked how long a man's legs should be: "Long enough to reach the ground."

There is no simple rule here. Mission statements need to be memorable. They should be as short as they can be in order to do the job at hand, but not so short as to be useless. Alcoa has a "vision statement" that calls on the company to be "the best company in the world." Well, that is certainly aspirational. But what does it mean? Best at what? A little more detail would be helpful, please.

In the discussion above, we've focused mostly on corporate mission statements. But that raises an important question: Does one mission statement suffice for a large, complex, modern corporation? Or do individual operating units need their own mission statements?

Our advice to managers is this: start by looking at the existing corporate mission statement, and any other relevant mission statements in the organization. If you think your group has a unique and somewhat separate mission that's not adequately captured in these broader statements, then proceed with your own. But proceed cautiously. Make sure whatever you do is consistent with the broader mission of the organization. Proliferating and conflicting missions within the same organization are a recipe for chaos.

When drafting a new mission statement, it's a good idea to involve as many people as possible. Remember that a key to your success is having the entire organization feel committed to a common goal. Members of the organization will feel more committed if they've had the opportunity to participate in defining that goal.

As a writer, however, I feel it's also important to warn of one pitfall that frequently trips up those writing mission statements. The statements can and should reflect contributions from numerous people. But they should never be written by committee. No great poem, no fine novel, no moving story, indeed nothing much worth reading, has ever been written by committee. Once you've decided what it is you want your mission statement to say, I'd recommend picking a good writer and sending him or her off to compose it. There's a reason the Second Continental Congress turned the writing of the Declaration of Independence over to Thomas Jefferson. Ben Franklin and others may have edited his work, refined some of his concepts, and eliminated some of his more excessive flourishes. But the Declaration still inspires us today because, in large part, it came from Jefferson's skilled pen.

STRATEGY

The word *strategy* has its origins in the military. A *strategus* was a commander in chief in ancient Greece; and *strategy* referred to the art of the commander in chief, directing the larger military movements and operations of a campaign. The classic text on military strategy, *The Art of War*, was written more than two thousand years ago, by a Chinese warrior-philosopher named Sun Tzu. Master Sun urged military strategists to assess both their own armies and their opponent's armies on five things before beginning a campaign. The five were: *the way*—a term Sun Tzu used to refer to the degree to which the people shared the goals of their leaders—the *weather*, the *terrain*, the *leadership*, and the *discipline*. Once the battle had begun, he said the military should follow five rules: *measurement, assessment, calculation, comparison,* and *victory*.

> The ground gives rise to assessments, assessments give rise to calculations, calculations give rise to comparisons, comparisons give rise to victories.

Not all organizational efforts, of course, are comparable to war. In war, if one side is to win, the other must lose. In business and other endeavors, there are ample opportunities for outcomes that benefit multiple participants. Yet the parallels are strong enough that books like Sun Tzu's *The Art of War* or Carl von Clausewitz's *On War* retain a key place on many business school reading lists. The disciplines of military strategy—assessing the opposition; surveying the playing field; making careful measurements, calculations, and comparisons; and thinking ahead, as if playing a game of multidimensional, multiplayer chess—are the same disciplines that are key to the success of any organizational strategy.

In business, strategy tends to focus on differentiation. Bruce Henderson, who founded the Boston Consulting Group, called strategy a "deliberate search for a plan of action that will develop a business's competitive advantage and compound it." Thus a company like eBay thrived by creating an entirely new way for people to buy and sell goods, and Dell computer beat out competitors by circumventing retail stores and selling via catalog.

A good strategy can bring about many years of success and profit. Southwest Airlines, for instance, became the darling of a highly competitive airline industry by charting a separate course characterized by low fares, good service, frequent departures, and point-to-point service at a time when the major airlines were developing hub-and-spoke systems.

Likewise, Intel's Andy Grove—who titled his memoirs with a modern adaptation of a Sun Tzu–like warning: *Only the Paranoid Survive*—set the company up for decades of prosperity by transforming it from a manufacturer of memory chips into the dominant producer of high value microprocessors.

A bad strategy, on the other hand, can lead to years of disaster. The *Journal* has chronicled the decades-long decline of a classic American business, Sears, Roebuck & Co., brought about by a 1981 decision to diversify into the financial business by purchasing the Dean Witter Reynolds securities brokerage business and the Coldwell Banker real estate operation, and later by launching the Discover credit card. The strategy, derided as "socks and stocks," proved disastrous. There was little or no synergy among the businesses—people didn't want to trade stocks or buy houses at a Sears store—and the multiple businesses caused the company to lose focus. As one analyst told the *Journal:* "No one watched the store." As Sears pursued its faulty one-stop shopping strategy, other retailers made inroads with specialty stores, allowing other companies to steal its traditional business.

The Sears retail business, now owned by financier Eddie Lampert, still hasn't recovered.

As a business discipline, the serious study of strategy is usually credited to a landmark book, *Competitive Strategy*, published in 1980 by Harvard Business School professor Michael Porter. Although it is thirty years old now, the book is still cited as the definitive text on the subject. Several members of *The Wall Street Journal* CEO Council cited it as the most influential business book they had read.

In the classical economist's view of the world, numerous players in a market compete against one another, driving prices down and quality up, and keeping profits modest. As Porter sees it, strategy is all about escaping that model of "perfect competition" and instead creating a strong position for your product or service that allows you to garner outsize profits.

Porter cites five key competitive "forces" that will determine the ability of your product or service to achieve a strong strategic position:

1. **Entry.** How easy is it for others to enter your market? Do newcomers face significant barriers, or do they expect sharp retaliation from existing competitors? Barriers to entry can include economies of scale, a highly differentiated product, large capital requirements for new entrants, large costs for customers to switch, limited access for newcomers to distribution channels, and government regulations or subsidies.

2. **Threat of substitution.** Are there other products and services that can easily be substituted for yours? Consider, for instance, what the rise of corn syrup did to the sugar industry, or what the iPod did to the CD business.

3. **Bargaining power of buyers.** Are a small number of buyers responsible for a large portion of your sales? Do their purchases from you represent a large portion of their costs? Can they easily switch suppliers, or go into your business themselves? Is your product relatively unimportant to the quality of their product or service? If the answer to these questions is yes, the buyer has significant leverage over you and your pricing.

4. **Bargaining power of suppliers.** Do you have multiple suppliers? Are there substitutes you can use? Is it easy to switch suppliers? Are you a relatively important customer? Is their product a relatively unimportant input for you? In this case, a yes answer means you have significant bargaining power over them.

5. **Rivalry among current competitors.** How intense is the rivalry among the firms you compete with? This will also affect your ability to sustain profits.

In coping with these five forces, Porter argues there are three generic strategies a firm can take to create superior profits:

- **Overall cost leadership.** If you keep your costs lower than anyone else's, you can sustain profits. This was the strategy of Dell computers, for instance, and Walmart.
- **Differentiation.** If you can create something that is valued as unique—think Mercedes, or Apple Computer—you can succeed in making more money than others in the industry.
- **Focus.** By focusing on the unique needs of a particular group of buyers, a particular geographic region, or a particular segment of the product line, you may be able to earn above-average returns.

Porter argues that it is critical that companies make clear strategic choices about their approach. The worst position, he argues, is to be "stuck in the middle," without either clear price leadership, a clearly differentiated product, or a distinct focus.

In recent years, many critics have argued that Porter's analysis is too static for a rapidly changing world. Strategic decisions based on the Porter framework will be constantly upended by changes in the marketplace, they argue.

We'll address these criticisms further in a later chapter, but it's worth mentioning here another influential book that grew out of the criticism called *Blue Ocean Strategy*, published by W. Chan Kim and Renee Mauborgne in 2005.

While avoiding use of Porter's name, Kim and Mauborgne nevertheless attack him head-on, arguing that the "five forces" analysis is a formula for remaining in "red oceans," where the sharks compete mercilessly for the action. The key to exceptional business success, they say, is to redefine the terms of competition and move into the "blue ocean," where you have the water to yourself. The goal of these strategies is not to beat the competition, but to make the competition irrelevant.

Among the examples they cite is Cirque du Soleil, the Canadian company that redefined the dynamics of a declining circus industry in the 1980s. Under conventional strategy analysis, the circus industry was a loser. Star performers had "supplier power" over the company. Alternative forms of entertainment, from sporting events to home entertainment systems, were relatively inexpensive and on the rise. Moreover, animal rights groups were putting increased pressure on circuses for their treatment of animals.

Cirque du Soleil eliminated the animals and reduced the importance of individual stars. It created a new form of entertainment that combined dance, music, and athletic skill to appeal to an upscale adult audience that had abandoned the traditional circus.

Instead of "five forces," Kim and Mauborgne talk about "four actions" that can help you create a blue ocean strategy. The actions are found by answering these questions:

- Which of the factors that the industry takes for granted should be eliminated? (In the case of Cirque du Soleil, that included animals, star performers, and the three separate rings.)
- Which factors should be reduced well below the industry's standard? (Cirque du Soleil reduced much of the thrill and danger associated with conventional circuses.)
- Which factors should be raised well above the industry's standard? (Cirque du Soleil increased the uniqueness of the

venue by developing its own tents, rather than performing within the confines of existing venues.)

- Which factors should be created that the industry has never offered? (Cirque du Soleil introduced dramatic themes, artistic music and dance, and a more upscale, refined environment.)

Kim and Mauborgne argue that businesses should focus less on their competitors and more on alternatives; they also should focus less on their customers, and more on noncustomers, or potential new customers.

More than a million copies of *Blue Ocean Strategy* have been sold. Marcelo Claure, chief executive of Brightstar Communications, recommended it to us, saying it has provided the "most value" of any business book he's read. "Teaching yourself to think constantly outside of the box and defining new strategies, even though some may fail, is a requirement for all CEOs," he said.

FORMULATING A STRATEGY

How do you formulate a strategy for your own organization? Following the lessons of Sun Tzu, Porter, and Kim and Mauborgne will certainly help. But for simplicity's sake, we offer this five-step process:

1. **Look outward: assess your organization's environment.** Who are the other players on your playing field? Who else may join in? What are the conditions you all face? Where are the opportunities that have yet to be exploited, and the risks waiting to be uncovered?
2. **Look inward: assess your organization's strengths and weaknesses.** What resources do you have or can you call on?

What capabilities does your group possess and what capabilities can it acquire? What are your inherent competitive advantages?

3. **Identify multiple threats and opportunities.** It's important that your strategic planning process look at all the possible alternatives for going forward, not just one. The process of careful analytic comparison will, in the end, help you make the wisest choices.

4. **Evaluate the effects of the strategies on all parts of your organization.** Even the smallest organization can be baffling in its complexity. Before settling on a strategy, you need to make sure you understand how it affects every aspect of the organization.

5. **Create alignment.** This is critical. You need to make sure everyone in your organization understands the strategy, understands his or her part in that strategy, and is in alignment with it. You should include as many people as possible in steps one through four, not only to benefit from their collective experience and knowledge, but also to help ensure alignment once the new strategy is chosen.

How often should you change strategies?

If your team's strategy is seen as ephemeral—shifting on the whim of top managers—then the team members' commitment to that strategy is likely to be ephemeral as well.

On the other hand, if you are unwilling to admit error when a strategy is clearly failing, or when circumstances demand change, then you may be doomed to follow the unfortunate path of, say, Sears, Roebuck.

For the skillful manager, strategy requires a bit of deception. You must show a firm commitment to your strategy in order to rally others around it. At the same time, you must always be willing privately to question your strategy when circumstances require it, and not let emotion or the fear of admitting error tie you to a failed approach. The effective manager needs to be at once both resolute, and open to new ideas and information.

Peter Drucker suggests this discipline: "Every three years, an organization should challenge every product, every service, every policy, every distribution channel with the question, If we were not in it already, would we be going into it now?"

In his book *Only the Paranoid Survive*, Andy Grove tells the story of how, as chief operating officer of Intel, he walked into the office of CEO Gordon Moore and asked the question: "What would a new management do if we were replaced?" The answer was clear: exit the business of memory chips, which had become a commodity business, and focus on microprocessors. That was almost unthinkable at the time, since Intel thought of itself as first and foremost in the computer memory business. But by switching to microprocessors, Grove and Moore cleared the way for Intel to enjoy decades of extraordinary success.

SETTING GOALS

Once your strategy is set, you can focus on the goals for your team and each of its members.

Here is where your role becomes critical. In many instances, you may have to accept the mission of the organization you work for, and you may have to support a strategy that has already been set by others. But setting goals is a critical part of every manager's job. Your group needs clear goals that can be met in a clearly articulated time frame. And every member of your group needs a set of personal goals, with clear deadlines or target dates attached.

As much as possible, you should involve members of your team in the goal-setting process. That serves two purposes. First, it allows you to tap the expertise and knowledge of others in the group. Second, it helps ensure alignment with the goals, once they are set.

There may be times when broad inclusion isn't possible. If you are trying to change an entrenched culture, for instance, and have little time in which to make the change, then you may choose to impose goals from the top down. But where possible, you're likely to get better long-term results by developing goals from the bottom up. Individual goals should be developed in consultation between the manager and the individual.

Our recommendation is that you write down clear goals for your organization, each subunit of the organization, and each individual in the organization, at least once every six months. To be effective, the goals should be:

- Clear and concise. You need to avoid ambiguity and unnecessary complexity.
- Recognized by everyone involved as important. If members of a team believe their goals are superfluous or trivial, they will act accordingly.
- Measurable. The old management adage that "you can't manage what you can't measure" endures because it is true. Many things are difficult to measure, but wherever possible, it's worth the effort.
- Framed in time. Where possible, goals should have a fixed deadline. If a deadline isn't possible, then they should at least have a clear time frame. Goals that aren't set in time are little better than no goals at all.
- Challenging, but achievable. This is a neat trick. You want to set goals that make people do their very best but at the same time are achievable. If the goal is set too high, it could prove discouraging and demotivating. If it is set too low, it could encourage mediocrity.

- Supported by the reward system. If a person's goal is to improve the quality of their output, but they are paid by the quantity, don't be surprised if the goal is ignored. If the goal is to improve a group's ability to work together as a team, but if people are singled out for praise based on individual effort, the goal again will be ignored.

In other words, while written goals are necessary to make an effective organization, they aren't sufficient. The goals have to be supported by the culture and actions of the entire organization.

TYING STRATEGY TO EXECUTION

In their book *The Strategy-Focused Organization*, Robert Kaplan and David Norton cite evidence that new strategies have failure rates "in the 70 to 90 percent range"—an extraordinary statistic, if true.

Why do well-formulated strategies fail?

One reason, Kaplan and Norton argue, is that the tools for measuring strategies haven't kept up with the pace of change. In the industrial economy, companies created value with their tangible assets—plant, equipment, and inputs like coal and steel. And most financial measurements, as you'll see in chapter 9, "Financial Literacy," later in this book, are based on tangible assets.

But in today's economy, value comes from intangible assets: customer relationships, innovative products and services, information technology and databases, powerful brands, and employee capabilities and motivations. These things don't show up clearly in an income statement or a balance sheet. As a result, they don't get fully accounted for in the budgeting and planning processes. And as we'll discuss in the next chapter, things that aren't measured tend not to be managed.

Thus the first step toward successful implementation of a strategy is adopting what Kaplan and Norton call a "balanced scorecard," which focuses on the most important goals of the strategy and develops measurements that track progress toward those goals. Those measurements are the key to translating strategy into meaningful operational terms.

Once measurements are in place, it's much easier to accomplish the critical task of communicating the strategy throughout the organization, and aligning individual performance with the strategy. Everyone in the organization should have a clear set of goals that map back to strategy, and should understand what their particular role in the strategy is. Their evaluations and incentives should be built around those strategic goals. As a result, strategy becomes part of everyone's everyday job.

Kaplan and Norton tell the story of Mobil Oil's transformation into a company that provided a higher quality service and experience to people at its gas stations. To do that, the company needed the buy in of the independent service station operators. Truck drivers delivering oil were told that part of their job, on which they were measured and compensated, was keeping service station operators feeling satisfied and happy. Because they understood the strategy, truck drivers also started reporting back to the company when they encountered a station that had dirty bathrooms or broken lights or was otherwise undermining the new strategy.

Ultimately, a successful strategy can't be a once-every-three-years exercise, but rather has to become a continual process. The strategy has to be reflected in budgets, in performance reviews, and in analytical and information systems. And there have to be ways for "strategic learning" to take place, as the organization sees how the strategy operates in practice.

In the end, strategy and *execution*, the topic of the next chapter, must become one and the same.

STRATEGY in Brief

- Managers must know where they are going and have a clear plan for getting there. If all you do is react to the demands and needs of others, you will fail.
- In setting strategy, you should identify multiple threats and multiple opportunities. If you settle on one approach too quickly, you are more likely to miss the big ones.
- Every member of your group needs to have a set of goals that are clear, measurable, and framed in time.
- In the end, strategy and execution must become part of the same process.

Further Reading

The Art of War, by Sun Tzu, Shambala, 1988. A classic that is still worth reading.

101 Mission Statements from Top Companies, by Jeffrey Abrahams, Ten Speed Press, 2007. This little book has good ones and bad ones but provides useful guidance if you are attempting to write your own.

Competitive Strategy, by Michael Porter, Free Press, 1980. This still has to be considered one of the most important business books ever written.

Blue Ocean Strategy, by W. Chan Kim and Renee Mauborgne, Harvard Business Press, 2005. A good antidote for those who feel Porter's book doesn't allow for the rapid pace of change in today's business world.

Strategy Is Destiny: How Strategy-Making Shapes a Company's Future, by Robert Burgelman and Andrew S. Grove, Free Press, 2001. An excellent look at strategy in action, written by one of my favorite Stanford professors.

The Strategy-Focused Organization, by Robert S. Kaplan and David P. Norton, Harvard Business Press, 2001. This is a detailed study on how to tie strategy to execution through the use of measurements, or what Kaplan and Norton call the "balanced scorecard."

I walk in many times and say "Okay, who's the chairman of this meeting?" It's quiet sometimes, so I just point someone out and say, "Okay, you're the chairman, take two or three minutes and do an agenda."

It causes them to have to think quick, prioritize quickly, and everybody is on their toes, 'cause they don't know when I'm going to walk in there and say, "Hey, you're going to be chair for the day."

T. BOONE PICKENS, *chairman, BP Capital Management, in a video interview for* The Wall Street Journal's *Lessons in Leadership series*

Chapter **SIX**

EXECUTION

Which is more important: Having the right strategy? Or executing well on that strategy?

That's been a widely debated question in business studies in recent years. The debate is a reaction to the rise of "strategy" as a key topic for study in business schools and a focus of attention among corporate leaders. Critics argue the focus on strategy has led some corporate leaders to spend too much time in ivory towers, charting their companies' courses, and too little time getting down and dirty in their organizations. Moreover, studies show far more strategies fail in their execution than succeed.

In their 2002 book, *Execution*, former AlliedSignal CEO Larry Bossidy and management consultant Ram Charan wrote: "Many people regard execution as detail work that's beneath the dignity of a business leader. That's wrong. To the contrary, it's a leader's most important job."

Bossidy, an ex-GE executive, says at the time he took over Allied-Signal in 1991, the company had "lots of hardworking, bright people, but they weren't effective, and they didn't place a premium on getting things done." The previous CEO, he says, saw his job as "buying and selling businesses," not building up the company's core processes.

Bossidy came in and instituted what he calls a "discipline of execution." Over the next eight years, operating margins tripled and shareholder returns increased ninefold. Other CEOs, says Charan, "placed too much emphasis on . . . high-level strategy, on intellectualizing and philosophizing, and not enough on implementation." Bossidy did the opposite.

We asked members of *The Wall Street Journal* CEO Council to weigh in on this debate. Which is the more important focus for a CEO: execution or strategy? The result was an interesting array of answers.

"If you have to elevate one over the other, I'd pick strategy," says Time Warner CEO Jeff Bewkes. "Mediocre execution of a great strategy probably will win more often than great execution of a mediocre strategy." Execution, several other CEOs argued, is more easily delegated to lower level employees, while strategy must be set by the CEO. "Ultimately, there are a lot of people who are delegated the responsibility of execution," said Lewis Hay, the CEO of FPL Energy.

But for every member of the council who gave the first nod to strategy, there was another who tipped the hat toward execution.

"Execution—it's not even close," said Russell Fradin, CEO of consulting firm Hewitt Associates. "If pushed to prioritize, I would say the scales tip to execution," agreed Jim Turley, CEO of Ernst & Young. "If I had to pick one over the other, I would pick execution," said Fred Tomczyk, CEO of TD Ameritrade. "Strategy is worth nothing if you can't execute it."

In this book, we take the view that the two are inseparably linked. Great strategy is pointless without great execution; and sterling execution gets you nowhere if you don't have the right strategy. Morris Chang, CEO of Taiwan Semiconductor Manufacturing Company, put it best: "Strategy and execution are equally important for a CEO. Without strategy, execution is aimless. Without execution, strategy is useless."

Ultimately, strategy and execution have to become part of the same process. "You can't separate the two," says WPP's Martin Sorrell.

A good example of a company that tried to separate the two, and failed, is the Boeing Company. After the merger between Boeing and McDonnell Douglas Corporation in 1997, McDonnell's Harry Stonecipher became president and chief operating officer, while Phil Condit remained chief executive officer.

Asked by the *Journal*'s Jeff Cole who was really in charge, Mr. Condit answered this way:

> Harry's job is chief operating officer. It is, "How are we doing?"
> Mine is chief executive. It is, "Where are we going?"

But Cole found it didn't really work that way. Stonecipher's relentless and hard-charging push for change rankled many old Boeing hands, who continued to see Condit as their defender. The two sides constantly found themselves pitted against each other. Even Condit acknowledged that there was a perception that it was "Harry and his army vs. Phil and his army." The result was Boeing continued to stumble. A 1999 survey showed even the company's own employees had sharply lower confidence that the company was making the changes necessary to stay competitive.

Other stories only reinforce the point. The person formulating the strategy also needs to be the person leading the execution. If "strategy" is deciding what to do, execution is all about making it happen. The two can't be separate.

The first three requirements for successful execution tie directly to the mission, strategy, and goal process discussed in the previous chapter. To have a strong culture of execution, you need: (1) clear goals for everyone in the organization, that are supportive of the overall strategy; (2) a means of measuring progress toward those goals on a regular basis; and (3) clear accountability for that progress. Those are the basics.

Beyond that, good execution requires constantly facing up to reality. An organization that executes well is one that is constantly staring the facts in the face. It doesn't spend a lot of time engaged in wishful thinking, or papering over problems, or trumpeting good news while hiding the bad. In a company with good execution, managers are constantly forcing the organization to face reality and deal with it.

You don't need an MBA to diagnose whether your organization has a strong culture of execution. It's usually obvious. Sit through a couple of management meetings, and you'll quickly get the idea.

If the meeting consists of a long PowerPoint presentation, filled with slides purporting to show all the wonderful things the presenting group has done; if others in the meeting sit quietly throughout, unwilling to ask questions or poke holes, knowing their own presentations will soon follow; if everyone leaves the meeting with no clear sense of what will happen next—then you have every reason to be concerned. This has all the hallmarks of a culture that tolerates poor performance.

On the other hand, if the presentation is short and to the point; if the presenter clearly highlights both successes *and* failures, opportunities *and* risks; if others feel free to question and debate the presentation; if there is a common understanding among everyone in the room on goals and timelines: and if all leave the room with a clear sense of what needs to happen next and who needs to do it, then you are likely witnessing a strong culture of execution.

Interestingly, it's not always the actions of the lead manager in the meeting room that signal the nature of the culture. If a manager sits silently through a long and uncritical and unquestioned presentation, he or she is probably failing to do the job. The same goes for a manager who raises questions or suggests goals that seem a total surprise to others in the room.

But if a manager sits silently as the presenter does a hard-headed critique; as others freely weigh in; and as everyone leaves with a clear sense of goals, timelines, and next steps, then the manager is doing the job. He or she has created a successful culture of execution that can govern itself.

Bossidy and Charan insist that creating such a culture has to be the top concern of the manager:

> Only the leader can set the tone of the dialogue in the organization. Dialogue is the core of culture and basic unit of work. How people talk to each other absolutely determines how well the organization will function. Is the dialogue stilted, politicized, fragmented, and butt-covering? Or is it candid and reality-based, raising the right questions, debating them, and finding realistic solutions? If it's the former—as it is in all too many companies—reality will never come to the surface. If it is to be the latter, the leader has to be on the playing field with his management team, practicing it consistently and forcefully.

Culture is a complicated concept. It means different things to different people. But for purposes of this chapter, we'll boil it down to two concepts that we believe are key to a successful organization: (1) a culture of *action,* and (2) culture of *candor.*

CREATING A CULTURE OF ACTION

Inertia is a great force in all organizations, as in nature. Things at rest have a tendency to remain at rest. A corollary of that physics property is this: it's usually easier to stop things from happening than it is to make them happen.

We've all seen this principle in operation. Someone comes into a room, excited about a new idea, and almost immediately others begin to pick it apart. "That's not our way of doing things." "We don't have the resources to do that." "We've *tried* that before." The most likely outcome: nothing changes.

That's why a key step in creating a successful culture of execution is creating a bias toward action. People who make things happen need to be praised and rewarded. People who don't should be coached to change, or weeded out. Failure cannot be unduly punished. Unless people feel free to make mistakes, they will not feel free to take bold actions.

In their book *In Search of Excellence*, Thomas Peters and Robert Waterman list a "bias for action" as the first of eight attributes that distinguish excellent and innovative companies. Many of the companies they studied were very "analytical in their approach to decision making, but they are not paralyzed by that fact (as so many others seem to be). In many of these companies, the standard operating procedure is: 'Do it, fix it, try it.'"

Peters and Waterman criticize most firms for their "overreliance on analysis from corporate ivory towers and overreliance on financial sleight of hand, the tools that would appear to eliminate risk but also, unfortunately, eliminate action." They talk of "paralysis through analysis"—driven in part by a business school culture that gives managers the tools to study, define, and analyze a problem but often not the leadership skills needed to convert understanding into action. They write:

Big companies seem to foster huge laboratory operations that produce papers and patents by the ton, but rarely new products. These companies are besieged by vast interlocking sets of committees and task forces that drive out creativity and block action. Work is governed by an absence of realism, spawned by staffs of people who haven't made or sold, tried, tasted, or sometimes even seen the product, but instead, have learned about it from reading dry reports produced by other staffers.

How do you create a bias for action? In large organizations, it often requires circumventing the bureaucracy. Rather than relegating new product ideas to the corporate planning staff, or assigning them to line managers who are already overburdened, the best companies create constantly shifting ad hoc project teams, task forces, project centers, or skunk works designed to get the job done.

We'll explore the dynamics of cross-functional teams in chapter 7. For our purposes here, though, the key is to encourage experimentation. A risk-averse team will analyze a new product or service to death before making a move. Instead, encourage the group to find a way to test the concept, at relatively low cost. Ready, fire, aim.

CREATING A CULTURE OF CANDOR

There are no silver bullets in the field of management. But insisting on candor comes as close to being an all-purpose problem solver as any idea we've encountered. There are many different terms for it—transparency, integrity, honesty, full disclosure, facing reality—but whatever you call it, it appears to be at the core of all great organizations.

The reason is that organizations, like people, have an endless ability to weave self-serving stories about themselves. And while such myth making may be critical to a person's, or an organization's survival, motivation, and self-esteem, it can often be destructive to results.

Collins calls this the "Stockdale paradox," after Admiral Jim

Stockdale, who was tortured repeatedly as a prisoner of war in the "Hanoi Hilton" during the Vietnam War. When asked by Collins how he survived his long ordeal, Stockdale replied that it was by never losing faith he would eventually get out. When asked who didn't survive, Stockdale replied that it was the "optimists"—the ones who thought, wrongly, they'd be out by, say, Christmas.

"This is a very important lesson," Stockdale told Collins. "You must never confuse faith that you will prevail in the end—which you can never afford to lose—with the discipline to confront the most brutal facts of your current reality, whatever they might be."

Great organizations exhibit a similar paradox. They are filled with people who are absolutely determined to see the organization succeed, whatever the odds against it. But they are also filled with people who are unstintingly honest in confronting the obstacles they face.

The first step toward creating a culture of candor is to ensure a free flow of information. That doesn't mean everyone needs to know everything; but it does mean that critical information must get to the right people at the right time and for the right reason.

"For any institution, the flow of information is akin to a central nervous system," write Warren Bennis, Daniel Goleman, and Patricia Ward Biederman in their book *Transparency: How Leaders Create a Culture of Candor.* "The organization's effectiveness depends on it. An organization's ability to compete, solve problems, innovate, meet challenges and achieve goals—its intelligence, if you will—varies to the degree that information flow remains healthy."

There are many reasons why the flow of information gets stunted in an organization. One widespread problem is the difficulty of "speaking truth to power." When speaking to their bosses, most people inevitably color the message—softening bad news, or spinning it in a way that's more likely to please. That can cause problems to go unaddressed.

Another problem is the tendency of managers to hoard information as a source of power. If they have it, and others don't, they can use that to justify their existence, or wield it selectively to achieve their own goals.

Sunk costs are yet another reason why people hinder the flow of information. If they've invested heavily in a project, they may be reluctant to pass on information showing that the project has problems, or is failing, and that the investment was a bad one.

To overcome these very natural human tendencies, managers must insist on candor at all times. They must reach out and solicit intelligence from as many people as possible. They must accept, and even welcome, troubling information when it's delivered to them, and praise those with the courage to surface unpleasant news. They must create systems designed to ensure good information flows to those who need it. And they must make it clear they are not interested in incessant happy talk.

SHOULD "MICROMANAGEMENT" BE AVOIDED?

As discussed above, a culture of execution requires you, as the manager, to be steeped in the details of your organization. But at what point does this immersion in details become the evil of "micromanagement"? Or, to put the problem in reverse, how do you keep your worries about micromanagement from preventing necessary attention to the details of execution?

There's no simple answer here. As a manager, you need to trust your subordinates to do the job you've asked them to do. If they feel you are breathing over their shoulders all the time, they'll inevitably become discouraged and disempowered and will perform poorly. It's hard to exercise judgment or initiative if you find yourself being second-guessed by your boss at every turn.

At the same time, you need to understand what's happening in the bowels of your organization, you need to ensure that goals and time-lines are being met, and you need to be prepared to take action when they aren't.

In the end, the answer to this seeming conundrum is the consistent practice of the principles discussed in the previous two chapters. To review:

- Set concrete goals in conjunction with your subordinates, so that you and they have a clear, common, and mutually accepted understanding of what needs to be done, in some detail.
- Make sure those goals are both attainable and measurable, and hold your subordinates accountable for their progress on a regular basis.
- Insist on a culture of action—rather than inaction, bureaucracy, "butt covering," or excessive analysis.
- Insist on a culture of candor, so you and your subordinates both know what's working, what isn't, and what the consequences are. Make sure information flows freely in both directions.

If you do these things, the "micromanagement" conundrum is likely to disappear. You'll have confidence that you know what's happening in the organization; and they'll know what they need to do to avoid the discomfort of being second-guessed.

EXECUTION in Brief

- Execution and strategy should be inseparable. Without strategy, execution is aimless. Without execution, strategy is useless.
- To have a culture of execution, you need: (1) clear goals for everyone; (2) a means of measuring progress toward those goals; and (3) accountability for that progress.
- Organizations that are good at executing tend to share two common traits: (1) a culture of action, and (2) a culture of candor.

Further Reading

Execution, by Larry Bossidy and Ram Charan, Crown Business, 2002. Bossidy's no-nonsense style, combined with Charan's analysis, make this the most popular, and most powerful, book on the topic.

Transparency: How Leaders Create a Culture of Candor, by Warren Bennis, Daniel Goleman, James O'Toole, with Patricia Ward Biederman, Jossey-Bass, 2008. Creating a culture of candor is as close as you'll get to finding a silver bullet in the management business.

In Search of Excellence, by Thomas J. Peters and Robert H. Waterman Jr., Harper and Row, 1982. A classic, somewhat out-of-date, but still worth reading.

The One Minute Manager, by Ken Blanchard and Spencer Johnson, Morrow, 1981. If you are looking for shortcuts, this one is as good as they get.

The whole BlackBerry user interface—the thing that makes it so simple to use and so responsive and gives you access to all these very complex things in a simple way—that was done through a committee. Believe it or not, it was done through a committee that I chaired over a period of ten years. And that committee was not just senior executives—it had coop students, it had interns, it had developers, it had tech writers, it had graphic artists. And it would change. We'd dynamically change the grouping depending on what problems we were trying to address. . . . That's the kind of culture we've built.

Mike Lazaridis, *Co-CEO, RIM,*
in an interview for The Wall Street Journal*'s*
Lessons in Leadership series

Chapter **SEVEN**

TEAMS

When Riley Tennant began working as a software-testing manager twenty years ago, organizing her employees was relatively simple. "You just decided things, and people went off and executed," she said.

But more recently, Tennant took a job at IBM managing engineers who customize database software for specific industries, such as financial services, government, and health care. She had four U.S.-based developers who reported directly to her, and three more based in China and India who did work for her but reported to managers in those countries.

After taking over, Tennant concluded she had too many people working on financial services, and not enough on government and health. But to shift resources, she had to persuade her peers thousands of miles away to go along with her plan. At first, the overseas managers resisted, fearing their local financial clients might lose out. Eventually they agreed, after Tennant promised to use other engineers to serve those clients when necessary.

These days, Tennant told my *Wall Street Journal* colleague Erin White, "Not everybody reports to you, and so there's much more negotiation and influence."

Tennant's challenge is becoming ever more common. In his research on middle managers, Paul Osterman found that "teams today are central to how work is done." In a complex world, they bring together people with disparate skills to solve complex problems—often people from different parts of the world or different parts of the organization.

"When I joined the company, one engineer could deliver a product, or at least the hardware side of it, by himself in many cases," a manager at a technology company told Osterman. "But I don't think we'll ever see that again in this company."

There are a number of reasons for this change. The increasing speed of technological change has pushed companies to create cross-functional teams that can tackle multiple tasks simultaneously, rather than sequentially. The increasing complexity of products and services means each task requires a greater array of knowledge and expertise. The emphasis on productivity has fed the growth of teams as a way of making more efficient use of workers, and reducing redundancy and slack. And globalization has increased the need for bringing workers from different geographies together on projects.

But teams have also caught on because they work. Think of the major challenges we've been talking about in this book. How do you motivate people to do their very best work? How do you get them to feel committed to their jobs? How do you tap their expertise and knowledge so you can be assured you are making the best decisions? A well-functioning team can be the answer to these questions.

Moreover, teams have become a powerful tool for avoiding the evils of bureaucracy. The best teams are established to take on a particular challenge and given a limited time to solve that challenge, and then they are disbanded. There's no permanent staff involved, no ongoing function for the group, and no opportunity for the group to become consumed with their own internal processes and self-perpetuation.

Teams have also upended traditional notions of management. Management theorists of the twentieth century began with the assumption that managers were overseeing a group of people who reported directly to them, whose pay they could control, and whom, at the end of the day, they could fire if necessary. But when working in cross-functional teams, managers frequently find that they have none of those traditional authoritarian tools.

We've argued throughout this book that modern management requires not just organizational skills, but also leadership skills; that the authority of managers comes not just from their formal position, but also from their ability to make work meaningful; and that the ultimate success of managers depends not just on telling workers what to do, but also on making them want to do it.

The rise of teamwork takes those developments one step further. If you are managing a team of people who don't report directly to you, the practices outlined in this book aren't just a good idea, they are essential to getting anything done. Your place in the hierarchy counts for nothing. Your ability to influence people counts for everything.

Odds are, if you've been in the workforce for a few years, you get the point. You may have been in a job where you were asked to head up a cross-functional task force, or where your success depended on your ability to get cooperation from a colleague in a different department, or where you had a great idea but had to get someone in a more senior position to buy on. In all of these situations, you have to rely on your ability to influence people over whom you have no authority.

Indeed the ability to make things happen without formal authority has become one of the most sought-after skills in today's workplace. The most-valued managers aren't those who have the most people reporting to them in the organization chart, but rather those who can best rally disparate workers to a common cause, or who can work well with peers toward a common goal.

How do you do that? The leadership and motivational skills discussed in chapters 2 and 3 are still at the core of the task. You need to understand what motivates the people you are working with and create a work environment that serves their needs.

But a growing body of business literature attempts to provide more specific guidance in how to manage teams and influence people who don't report to you. And many companies, such as IBM, have started providing employees with influence-skills training for their managers.

INFLUENCING COLLEAGUES

Remember that the workplace, at its core, is a marketplace. You give your labor, you get pay, benefits, and job satisfaction in return. You expend extra effort and creativity, and you get the praise of your boss, a renewed sense of purpose, the pride of a job well done, and perhaps a promotion.

Cross-functional teams are no different, except that as a manager, you've lost some of your trading currency. You can no longer directly influence a worker's pay, or provide them a promotion. So you have to find other things you can provide in exchange for their cooperation on a project.

For starters, you can provide meaning, the most important and least costly of currencies. As discussed in chapter 3, most modern workers seek fulfillment in their work. If you can show that the task at hand has larger significance for your unit, your organization, or for society, you can inspire others to join. People want to be involved in projects that matter. They like to be around others striving for excellence. If you can provide that inspirational vision, you may find others clamoring to join.

Beyond that, you should consider the individual needs of each person you are trying to enlist. Do they need new resources? Perhaps you control budget, people, or space that can suit their needs. Are they trying to expand their base of experience? Perhaps you can offer them the opportunity to increase their skills. Are they looking for support within the organization to accomplish other tasks? Perhaps you can provide that in exchange for their cooperation.

Moreover, while you don't directly control their pay and promotion within the organization, you can certainly offer to influence it. You can provide public recognition for a job well done, and enhance their reputation internally. You can recommend them for promotion or a pay raise, and make sure others are aware of their contributions.

Finally, there are more personal currencies, not to be overlooked. People work harder for people they like. They seek support, acceptance, inclusion, understanding, even friendship. They appreciate the gratitude of others. Relationships in the workplace are always important; but when you are trying to exercise influence without authority, they become critical. Time spent nurturing those relationships, in the lunchroom, at the watercooler, or even over a beer after work, is not time wasted. In the end, it may prove your most valuable currency.

So far in this section, we've been discussing positive trades— rewards, in effect, for encouraging cooperation. But inevitably you'll find situations where some workers simply refuse to cooperate, regardless of your best efforts. In those cases, you may have to take a different approach and play hardball, raising the cost to them of their failure to cooperate.

Perhaps you'll have to appeal to their boss, or to their boss's boss. Or enlist others in your effort to pressure them. Such negative tactics should be used only as a last resort, since they run the risk of hardening the uncooperative workers' resistance.

At the extreme, there may be times when you have to put your own job on the line. In their book *Influence without Authority*, Allan Cohen and David Bradford use the example of Donna Dubinsky, who was then at Apple Computer and later became CEO of Handspring and Palm. A group of executives, including Apple founder Steve Jobs, were pressuring her to change to a just-in-time inventory system that she was certain was inappropriate for Apple's business. She told company executives that she would resign if she weren't allowed to make the decision on her own. Ultimately, Apple president John Sculley agreed to her terms.

Needless to say, such threats must be used sparingly. But there are times when a calculated confrontation may be the only way to achieve results.

WHEN TO USE A TEAM

Teams are most valuable when you need to harness the skills and creativity of a diverse group of people to solve a particular challenge.

They aren't the right approach for every cross-functional challenge. Building a well-functioning team can be slow, inefficient, and time-consuming. When the task at hand is clear-cut and time is of the essence, you will be better off using a traditional, single-leader approach. Give one person the authority to map out the work, divide up the tasks, and get the job done.

But if the task is less clear, and you want to tap the collective skills and creativity of people from different departments and disciplines to find the best solution, then a team may be the right way to go.

Step one is to define the challenge. It needs to be clear and specific enough that each member of the team can understand it, get enthused about it, and get committed to it. At the same time, it must allow the team significant scope for creative action. If you're assembling a team to solve a problem, but then you outline the solution in your initial challenge, you probably shouldn't be using a team to begin with.

The team challenge should be focused on a specific outcome—regain lost market share among teenagers, or develop a compelling version of our service for mobile phones, or solve a knotty supply chain issue. It should *not* call for some sort of bureaucratic work product—a lengthy report on why we've lost teenage market share, for instance. Remember that your challenge as a manager is to create meaning for people. If the team challenge is clearly a meaningful one, you've passed the first test.

TEAM BUILDING

The next step, of course, is making sure you've got the right people on the team.

It's important that there be neither too many team members—a recipe for chaos—nor too few—a guarantee that some critical perspective is forgotten. The right number will depend on the circumstances, but in most cases, ten to twelve should be an absolute maximum. Anything larger becomes unwieldy.

It's also important that team members have the right amount of authority, but not too much. If members of the team are too senior in the organization, they may feel the project is not a good use of their time. If they are too junior, they may not have the authority to ensure the project's success. If you are going to err, err on the side of more seniority rather than less, since insufficient authority dooms more projects than the opposite.

Finally, it's critical that every member of the team be prepared to make a major, positive contribution to the project. A common problem occurs when people sign up for teams because they feel they "deserve" to be on them, rather than because they need or want to be on them.

Even more destructive are those who sign up for defensive reasons—they want to make sure the team doesn't head down a path that could harm a separate project.

And remember—teams take time and work. It may be possible for someone to serve on two or even three teams at the same time, but probably not more than that. They need to commit going in to devote significant time to the challenge.

THE ROLE OF THE TEAM LEADER

A key to a team's success is a sense of mutual accountability. Members of the group need to feel they will succeed or fail as a group—and not worry that some individual—particularly the team leader—will claim all the credit for the group's work.

That makes the leader's role particularly challenging. As leader, you will have to devote a good deal of time to making sure the right culture exists within the team. This is where team-building exercises, while sometimes taken to silly extremes, can serve a purpose. You're likely to have little direct authority over the members of your team. And even if you do have some authority, you've got to be careful exercising it, as it will undercut the team ethos.

Still, team leaders do have an important set of tools of influence in their hands, for one key reason: they control the process. And process is power.

You should start by assembling a project charter. What is the challenge that the team is being asked to solve? What is the scope of the project? What are the benefits? What are the specific goals that have to be met, and the timetable for meeting those goals? What are the dependencies on other projects, the high-level risks, and other significant issues?

These aren't questions you should answer on your own. Rather they are questions that need to be answered by the team. But as team leader, you are in a position to insist they be answered at the outset. By doing so, you can make sure all members of the group agree on the task at hand.

Then carefully delineate who has responsibility for what. Make sure each person signs up for specific responsibilities and timetables. And make sure those responsibilities and timetables are expressed in as clear language as possible. As team leader, you should insist on clarity and specificity; don't allow team members to get by making only vague commitments. The following exchange from a *Dilbert* cartoon demonstrates the kind of discussion to be avoided:

> TEAM LEADER: Wally, you've agreed to pull together all of the technical specifications by Thursday, right?
>
> WALLY: Yes, I'll look into pulling that stuff together.
>
> TEAM LEADER: I don't need you to "Look into it." I need you to do it.
>
> WALLY: I agree.
>
> TEAM LEADER: Are you agreeing that I need it or agreeing to do it?
>
> WALLY: You will have the list of who has the technical specifications by Thursday.
>
> TEAM LEADER: I don't need the list of who has them. I need the specifications!
>
> WALLY: I agree.
>
> TEAM LEADER: GAA!!! Forget it! I'll get them myself!

Once the project is started, you, as team leader, also control the measurement of the project. Are tasks being completed on time and on budget? It's worth keeping careful track of this, so everyone sees problems as soon as they arise. How does the project timing compare to plan? How does spending compare to budget? Which pieces of the project have stoplight "red" or "yellow" indicators attached? How much has the scope of the project changed since it began? How much time has been invested, compared to budget? Remembering again that what isn't measured likely won't be managed makes the task of team management much simpler.

As team leader, you also need to keep careful track of the scope of the project. "Scope creep" often causes projects to derail. But a well-defined scope for the project, and a clear process for handling, and if necessary rejecting, proposals to change the scope, can prove powerful tools in keeping teams on track.

Inevitably, of course, problems will arise. You may have a team member who faces conflicting priorities and insufficient time to do them all. You may find necessary resources or information for one part of the project are delayed. Or you may have a team member who simply doesn't have the ability or the motivation to do the necessary work. When that happens, it's best to start with a candid conversation with the team member, asking for suggestions on how to handle the problem. If the problems persist, you'll have to turn to the manager who does have direct authority. But if you've handled the rest of the team process well, those instances will be rare.

TEAM DECISION MAKING

Making decisions in a team poses special challenges. The autocratic approach—"I'm the team leader, so I decide"—undercuts the whole purpose of having a team. As mentioned above, it may work in situations where the task is fairly clear-cut and time is of the essence. But even then, team leaders who take the autocratic leadership approach may soon find no one is following.

The key to a successful team effort is unity of purpose. To achieve and maintain that kind of unity, consensus building is best. If a consensus can been reached, everyone in the group will understand the decision and be prepared to support it. Moreover, a consensus decision is more likely to be the right decision.

But consensus building is hard. It can take an inordinate amount of time, and in today's fast-moving world, time often isn't practical. Moreover, some decisions involve deeply held differences among team members, making consensus impossible.

So if consensus isn't possible, how should decisions be made? There's no simple answer, and every approach has its pluses and minuses. Some common approaches include:

The democratic approach. Allowing the team to vote will usually be accepted as a reasonable way to proceed. But it doesn't always guarantee the all-critical unity of purpose. If team members of the losing side feel strongly about the decision, they may lose commitment to the project. And in the future, it will be all too easy for them to blame project problems and failures on the faulty decision by the majority. Moreover, not all important decisions are binary. If the team faces three or four different options, it may not be possible to reach a majority decision.

The plurality approach. If there are multiple options, the group may decide to go with the one that receives the most votes, even if not a majority. This is an especially dicey route, since now a majority of team members have expressed opposition to the approach taken. Moreover, it's an approach that seldom leads to the best decision.

Defer to the experts. Let's face it, not everyone on your team has the same knowledge about every decision that has to be made. So why not defer to the experts in the group? If it's a decision about which technology to use, let the technologists decide. If it has to do with a marketing approach, let the marketers decide.

This doesn't mean team members should refrain from vigorously expressing their opinions on matters outside their expertise. That's the value of the team approach: getting input from various perspectives. But if consensus can't be reached, it may make sense, at the end of the day, to defer to those who know the most.

The consultative approach. The successful team leader can't be an autocrat. But if the leader fully consults with all members of the team, listens carefully, and takes all views into account, he or she may be able to make an informed decision on a path forward that's accepted by the rest of the team as valid.

The one thing this chapter should make clear is that leading a team of people over whom you have no direct authority takes a lot of time and energy. You have to work on building and maintaining your relationship with every member of the team. Shortcuts, while often tempting in the rush to complete a project, can lead to disastrous problems down the line. There are plenty of examples of a single disgruntled team member causing a project to implode. That's a risk you can't afford.

A good rule of thumb is that you'll have to spend 10 percent of your time with each key member of a team. That means if the team has ten members, keeping it on track will be a full-time job. Don't be fooled into thinking you can be the player-coach—both leading the project and being a fully functioning participant. If it's a big team, you likely can't.

TEAMS in Brief

- Cross-functional teams have become the standard operating unit in many modern workplaces.
- Ten people should be the maximum for any team, and each member should be prepared to make a significant contribution of time.
- Teams need a clearly defined challenge and a finite time frame. When the task is done, they should be disbanded.
- Managing a team takes time. Assume you'll have to spend as much as 10 percent of your time with each team member.

Further Reading

The Wisdom of Teams, by Jon R. Katzenbach and Douglas K. Smith, Collins Business, 2006. This is the best book I've found on the why and how to use teams to improve organizational performance.

Influence without Authority, by Allan R. Cohen, David L Bradford, John Wiley and Sons, 2005. A solid academic work, but a bit too theoretical and jargon filled for my taste.

Results without Authority, by Tom Kendrick, American Management Association, 2006. This is a more tactical book that shows how to use control of the team process to gain control of the project.

Influence, by Robert B. Cialdini, HarperCollins, 1984. A classic text by a social psychologist about how to influence people, for good or for ill.

I took over Xerox in 2000. I had been with Xerox for thirty-four years, but I became president in 2000. It was an extraordinary time for the company. We were in deep crisis. So there was no choice but to be on a journey of extraordinary change.

It's one of the benefits of actually having a crisis. It does give you permission to challenge all areas of the business.

ANN MULCAHY, *former CEO, Xerox,*
in a video interview for The Wall Street Journal's
Lessons in Leadership series

Chapter **EIGHT**

CHANGE

At *The Wall Street Journal,* we sit in the midst of an industry going through breathtakingly rapid change.

The majority of our readers no longer find us waiting for them as a folded paper on their doorstep or at the end of their driveway each morning. Instead, they access us by computer or a mobile device, at any time of the day or night. Many visit us using services—Google, Facebook, Twitter—that didn't exist a decade ago.

Hundreds of thousands of them read us on small devices that they carry around in their pockets or briefcases or purses—devices like the BlackBerry, the iPhone, the Kindle, the iPad—with new and improved versions being brought to market almost every month. They not only read us but also watch us on video and listen to us on podcasts. They enjoy our interactive graphics and look at our extensive slide shows and research topics that particularly interest them. And they talk back! Thousands of them comment on our articles every day, providing rich strings of analysis that are often as interesting, or more interesting, than the stories themselves.

In the process, these changes have upended traditional business models. Proud old newspapers of the twentieth century have found themselves in bankruptcy—the *Los Angeles Times,* the *Chicago Tribune,* the *Philadelphia Inquirer*, the *Minneapolis Herald Tribune*, the *New Haven Register*. Others, such as the *Christian Science Monitor* and the *Seattle Post-Intelligencer*, have shut down their print editions altogether. Still others, such as the Detroit papers, are limiting home delivery to just a few days a week.

Nearly all are struggling financially. The *New York Times* had to turn to the richest man in Mexico, Carlos Slim, in order to find financial support. At one point in 2009, a share of stock in the McClatchy Company actually cost less than a single copy of many of the papers it publishes.

Yet here's the remarkable thing: as I talk to CEOs around the world today, I find the pace of change in our industry is not seen as an exception, but rather as the rule. Most industries seem to be going through major changes, at a rapid pace. That's certainly true of finance, technology, any industry that is powered by fossil fuels, or any that relies on the dissemination of information, or any that might benefit from artificial intelligence or the mapping or the human genome, or any that could be affected by rapid development in third world markets. Change is everywhere, fast and furious.

In a survey of 1,130 CEOs conducted in 2008, IBM found that 83 percent of them said their companies faced "substantial" or "very substantial" change over the next three years. That was up from 65 percent just two years earlier. Many of them admitted they were struggling just to keep up. A Canadian CEO likened his job to white-water rafting.

There are a number of reasons for this. The business world, for one, has become much more global and much more competitive. The last quarter of the twentieth century witnessed a huge shift toward markets-oriented economics around the world, with communism and socialism collapsing and governments everywhere loosening their grips on economic activity. In many developing countries—China, India, Brazil—

growth exploded as a result. In such a world, any company that doesn't keep pace with change can quickly find itself lapped by competitors.

Technology is also a major driver. Gordon Moore, the cofounder of Intel, is famous for observing that since the invention of integrated circuits—computer chips—in 1958, the number of transistors that can be placed on an integrated circuit has increased exponentially, doubling every two years. Other technologists, like Ray Kurzweil, extrapolate that trend across all technologies:

> An analysis of the history of technology shows that technological change is exponential, contrary to the common-sense "intuitive linear" view. So we won't experience 100 years of progress in the twenty-first century—it will be more like 20,000 years of progress (at today's rate). The "returns," such as chip speed and cost-effectiveness, also increase exponentially. There's even exponential growth in the rate of exponential growth.

A popular video circulating on the Internet these days captures the trend by looking at how long it took various consumer innovations to reach fifty million people:

> Radio—thirty-eight years
> Television—thirteen years
> Internet—four years
> iPod—three years
> Facebook—two years

The implications of this for managers of organizations of all types are profound. How do you make or execute strategic plans in a world where everything is changing so rapidly? How do you set a clear direction for your organization when, like the Canadian CEO, you feel you are riding in white water and need to devote all your energies to just making sure you aren't turned upside down by the chaotic churn of the waters?

Indeed, for many organizations, the accelerating pace of change raises an existential question. Organizations are devoted to continuity; they exist to perpetuate themselves. But technology and markets are forces of discontinuity, or what the economist Joseph Schumpeter referred to as "creative destruction." It's no accident that as change has accelerated, the expected life span of corporations has declined. Decades-old giants like Bear Stearns and Lehman Brothers can disappear overnight, while new ones with funny names like Google and Twitter spring up from seemingly nowhere. It's telling that only 86 of the companies in the S&P 500 stock index were there when the index was started in 1957.

You begin to wonder whether the corporation—one of the most successful innovations of the twentieth century—isn't on its way to becoming a victim of innovation in the twenty-first. We'll put that question aside until the end of this chapter. In the meantime, we'll address how managers should, and shouldn't, deal with the galloping pace of change.

DEALING WITH CHANGE

The demise of General Motors, once the largest and most successful automaker in the world and now a ward of the U.S. government, is an object lesson in how difficult it can be for organizations to face change.

Even the most casual observers of mighty GM have known for nearly four decades that the auto giant was in need of radical restructuring. The rise of Japanese competition made it clear that the company's labor contracts were far too cushy, its dealer network was way too large and diverse, and its manufacturing and design methods were outdated.

Most outside observers also recognized that at the center of all these other problems was a Motor City culture that was too proud, too insular, and too resistant to change to serve the industry well.

Over the years, there have been efforts to effect change. My *Wall Street Journal* colleagues Joe White and Paul Ingrassia won a Pulitzer for their coverage of a remarkable boardroom drama in 1992, when a pair of outsiders—former Procter & Gamble chairman John G. Smale and his advising attorney, Ira Millstein—attempted to remake the company's management.

Smale was a GM director in an era when outside directors were supposed to be seen but rarely heard—or at least rarely listened to. In those days, the notion that a group of outside directors would unseat a chief executive—a practice that has become much more common since the turn of the century—was virtually unheard of.

But Smale and his fellow outside directors had lost patience with CEO Robert Stempel's plodding efforts to address the carmaker's profound problems. Stempel was an affable "car guy," popular with employees but hardly the change agent that the company needed.

In March of 1992, Smale and his fellow outside directors summoned Stempel to a secret meeting near O'Hare Airport in Chicago. They told him he wasn't moving fast enough to cure the company's ills. Then they directed him to dump two of his top senior executives and to step down from the chairmanship of the board's executive committee, letting Smale himself assume the post.

In October, the standoff grew more tense, as rumors began to spread that the board wanted Stempel out. The CEO asked Smale to put out a statement quashing the rumors. Instead, Smale issued a terse statement that was as piercing as a knife: GM's board, he said, "continues to reflect upon the wisest course for assuring the most effective leadership for the corporation." Rather than be pushed out, Stempel quit, clearing the way for John F. Smith to take the reins.

At the time, the boardroom revolt was seen by outsiders as a welcome harbinger of the change GM needed. But it wasn't. Indeed, one of the people elevated in the coup was Richard Wagoner, age thirty-nine, who became executive vice president and chief financial officer. Fourteen years later, Wagoner found himself in the same fix Stempel had once been in, with most of the needed change still waiting to happen.

As my colleague Monica Langley reported, Wagoner learned that outside board members were about to hold a special board meeting without him. Speculation was rampant that his job was at risk. Taking advice from his predecessor, John F. Smith, he went to the board and demanded a vote of confidence, threatening to resign if he didn't get it. The board gave it to him.

But the fact that he needed a vote of confidence to survive was signal enough that his days were numbered. In 2009, by the time the government stepped in, it was clear Wagoner had to go. More important, it was clear that General Motors had failed to heed the alarm bells that had been ringing around it for the previous four decades and was destined for a much more modest future.

Why couldn't General Motors make the changes that so obviously needed to be made? Its story is common enough that the question deserves, and has gotten, serious study. For every tale of an IBM, which transformed itself under the leadership of Louis Gerstner, there are ten stories of companies like General Motors, which didn't.

The *Journal*'s John Keller, for instance, followed the downward slide of the once iconic AT&T Inc. Telecom deregulation had put the company's long-distance business under attack from both regional telephone companies—the so-called Baby Bells that had once been part of AT&T before a court-ordered breakup—and from new entrants like WorldCom and Sprint. Recognizing the need for change, CEO Robert Allen brought in a fast-moving printing executive, John R. Walter, to be president and chief executive-in-waiting.

Walter wasted no time shaking the business up. He centralized control of the company's business units, and began striking friendly deals with the rival Baby Bells, rather than trying to compete with them in the local phone market. He summarily removed one of the company's top executives, declaring "no individual is indispensable." And he teasingly referred to the company's spacious and cushy executive offices where the remaining senior executives worked as "Carpet Land," saying it took so long to cross the space that "by the time I get to somebody's office, I forget why I was going there."

Unlike GM's John Smith, John Walter was determined to drive change. But barely eight months later, he was fired. Allen, bruised by Walter's sharp elbows, convinced the board that he wasn't showing the "intellectual leadership" to be CEO. AT&T, like GM, never changed. In 2005, the hobbled giant was bought by SBC Communications Inc., one of the Baby Bells, which took its iconic name.

DISRUPTIVE CHANGE

It's easy to attack GM and AT&T as hidebound dinosaurs whose slow-moving sclerosis was the result the oligopolistic or monopolistic positions they had once enjoyed in the marketplace.

But in his book *The Innovator's Dilemma*, Harvard professor Clayton Christensen shows how even many of the best, most competitive corporations have succumbed to similar fates when faced with what he calls "disruptive" innovation.

IBM dominated the mainframe computer business but totally missed the emergence of minicomputers. That revolution was led by Digital Equipment Corporation—the subject of Tracy Kidder's *The Soul of the New Machine*—which then totally missed the move to personal computers. Apple Computer helped lead the way on personal computers but fell far behind on portable computers. And so it goes.

Christensen says similar stories can be told about dominant companies missing the move in telephones (from landlines to mobile), in printing (offset to digital), in photography (film to digital), in stock brokerages (full service to online), stock exchanges (floor to electronic networks), and retailing (brick-and-mortar to online). Even graduate schools of management, he argues, were too slow to address the rise of corporate universities and in-house management training.

In an interesting analysis, Christensen argues that companies fail at dealing with these challenges not because of bad management, but because of what once would have been viewed as good management. By listening closely to their customers, for instance, they missed innovations that had little appeal to current customers but opened up whole new categories of customers. By carefully studying market trends and allocating investment capital to the innovations that promised the largest returns, they missed disruptive changes that carried lower margins. Writes Christensen:

> What this implies at a deeper level is that many of what are now widely accepted principles of good management are, in fact, only situationally appropriate. There are times at which it is right not to listen to customers, right to invest in developing lower-performance products that promise lower margins, and right to aggressively pursue small, rather than substantial, markets.

Christensen ends by offering six tips for dealing with the possibility of disruptive change, which are summarized below:

1. **The customer isn't always right.** While it clearly pays to listen closely to your customers and clients, don't expect them to help you spot disruptive innovations. You'll need other forms of intelligence to help you do that.

2. **Resource allocation is key.** Once you think you've spotted a potential disruptive innovation, you'll have to make special efforts to allocate resources to develop it. Traditional models that measure return on investment may not do the trick. That's a big reason why established companies often steer clear. You'll need a different approach for funding these investments, which may not look like they make sense in the early years.

3. **Disruptive technologies need new markets.** Don't try to force the disruptive technology into the demands of your existing market; instead look for new markets that value the characteristics of the new technology.

4. **Disruptive technologies may require new capabilities.** Being the leader in minicomputers may not mean you have the skills you need to be the leader in personal computers. To tackle a disruptive technology, you may need new people and new capabilities.

5. **Experiment.** Don't make big, expensive bets on unproven technology. Instead, try to make fast, inexpensive forays into new products and markets, and learn from the experience. Be prepared to fail before you succeed.

6. **Don't try to lead in every technology.** Disruptive technologies do often confer big advantages on the first mover. But what Christensen calls "sustaining technologies"—technologies that enhance an existing product and market—often do not.

One company that frequently wins praise for managing its way through this technological minefield is Cisco Systems Inc. In a front-page *Journal* story in 2000, management editor Scott Thurm painted a portrait of how Cisco has developed a system of buying smaller companies with promising technologies in order to maintain its dominance in networking equipment and systems.

The company has well-trained SWAT teams that move in even before a deal is inked to oversee the smaller company's assimilation. Workers are assured they will keep their jobs, and they often find their benefits improve. The whole system is designed to ensure that Cisco keeps the innovative portion of the new company's business, while fully integrating the newcomer into the parent. Between 1993 and 2000, Thurm found, Cisco had used this system to digest fifty-one different companies. And when the Internet bubble burst that year, taking down less skillful companies, Cisco's finely tuned process enabled it to survive and thrive.

MANAGING THROUGH CHANGE

Many of the management techniques already discussed in this book will help you manage in an environment of rapid change.

Empowering your employees or team members to make decisions, instead of concentrating decision making at the top, will help ensure coming changes are quickly spotted and addressed, since your employees are usually "closer to the ground" than you are and more likely to see big changes coming. Including employees in discussions about strategy and goals also helps, for the same reason. Creating a culture of candor will ensure that potentially threatening developments get surfaced quickly and are fully discussed. Creating a culture of action will ensure those changes aren't long ignored. Using ad hoc teams will enable you to quickly put together the right group of people to address new developments, without getting bogged down in processes and structures that were built for a different time and situation.

But inevitably, the day is likely to come when you will find yourself in a situation like that which faced John Walter of AT&T, or John Smith at GM. You will realize that a major change in approach is needed. And it will be up to you, as a manager, to make it happen.

That's no easy task, particularly when it involves changing an ingrained corporate culture. As a manager, you may have the power to change your organization's policies with the stroke of a pen. And you may have the ability to hire, fire, promote, and demote people with relatively little effort. But changing an entrenched culture is the toughest task you will face. To do so, you must win the hearts and minds of the people you work with, and that takes both cunning and persuasion.

Ford CEO Alan Mulally faced that problem square on when he became CEO of Ford after working at Boeing and General Electric. My colleague Monica Langley, who chronicled his early days, says he instituted weekly Thursday meetings as the centerpiece of his plans for change. He banned cell phones, BlackBerrys, side conversations, mean jokes, personal opinions, turf battles, and bathroom breaks (unless urgent). In their place, he insisted on candor, data, results, more data, and applause for executives who showed progress.

Mulally quickly learned that Ford managers were in the habit of not sharing information with one another. As a result, reports from the individual unit heads didn't always add up. Mulally quickly insisted that change. "Data can set you free," he said. "You can't manage a secret."

Early on, when one manager described some poor performance in his unit, Mulally stunned the others by applauding in response. "Great visibility," he said. His point was clear: problems have to be surfaced before they can be solved.

The lessons learned by Mulally and others in managing change suggest a number of fundamental approaches that are necessary for success. They include:

Create an understanding of the need for change. Members of the organization need to know why change is necessary; otherwise, they are likely to stick stubbornly to old ways. Larry Summers's failure to transform the culture of Harvard was due in large part to the fact that the majority of the Harvard faculty didn't see any reason why their culture had to change.

Look outward. Perhaps the most important thing A.G. Lafley did to transform stodgy Procter & Gamble into a more innovative firm was to establish a goal that 50 percent of P&G's new product and technology innovations should come from outside the company. By doing so, he forced his people to reach out, find out what others had to offer, and not assume they had all the answers in-house.

Shift resources toward change. As discussed above, this is sometimes the hardest thing to do, because existing projects will always demand resources, and the new projects won't always offer clear returns. You've got to make sure resources are available for projects that help drive change.

Build a guiding coalition. You likely won't have the time or energy to convert everyone in the organization to your cause, so start with a key coalition of people who have disproportionate influence in the organization. And get rid of those who have disproportionate influence and can't be converted.

Look for ways to demonstrate the need for change. In Blue Ocean Strategy, Kim and Mauborgne tell the story of New York Police Commissioner Bill Bratton, who in the 1990s made his top brass— including himself—ride the subways day and night, to understand why frightened New Yorkers had come to call it the "Electric Sewer." Other companies have taken a similar approach, requiring managers to take calls from disgruntled customers.

Find a consigliere. Even the most perceptive of leaders has blind spots, especially when surrounded by people who are determined to keep him or her relatively content. You need at least one person at your side who knows who is supporting you, who is quietly fighting against you, and who can help you build coalitions and devise strategies for driving change.

The best-read book on this subject is *Leading Change* by John Kotter, who also authored the business penguin parable *Our Iceberg Is Melting*. Kotter cites the eight top reasons, from his research, why change efforts fail. Though in this management guide we generally like to dwell on what you should do, not on what you shouldn't, Kotter's list is instructive. The eight are paraphrased below:

Error 1: Complacency. The biggest mistake people make when trying to change organizations is to plunge ahead without establishing a high enough sense of urgency in fellow managers and employees. Do that, and you are likely to fail.

Error 2: Lack of allies. Before launching a big organizational transformation, you need a core group of allies—people who share your commitment to change. It doesn't have to include all your senior people, but it helps, as mentioned above, to include people with disproportionate influence.

Error 3: Lack of a uniform vision. A clear vision helps to both inspire and align the efforts of a large group of people. Without it, your transformation could dissolve into a list of projects with no clear direction.

Error 4: Undercommunicating the vision. As a manager, you learn quickly how often you have to repeat ideas before they are truly grasped by your employees. You need to be compelling and repetitive in communicating the vision, and you need to make sure your actions don't contradict your words.

Error 5: Letting obstacles get in the way. New initiatives inevitably run up against huge obstacles. To keep change moving, you must show you are willing to act quickly and forcefully to remove such obstacles.

Error 6. Failing to create short-term wins. Change

takes time, but you need to create short-term wins along the way to give your team a sense of progress.

Error 7. Declaring victory too soon. It's tempting, when you see substantial progress toward your goal, to declare the change a success. Don't do it. Celebrate your short-term wins, but try to avoid the mistake President Bush made when he appeared on the aircraft carrier during the early months of the Iraq war under a giant banner that said Mission Accomplished.

Error 8: Failing to anchor changes in the organizational culture. It's not enough to get rid of the old culture; you've got to create a new one. As Kotter puts it: "In the final analysis, change sticks only when it becomes 'the way we do things around here.'"

THE FUTURE OF MANAGEMENT

As I mentioned earlier in this chapter, the rapid pace of change is a challenge to the very existence of modern corporations and organizations.

British economist Ronald Coase laid out the logic for modern corporations in his 1937 work, *The Nature of the Firm.* He started with the basic question: Why do we need corporations? Classical economists envisioned a world in which individuals contracted with one another in the marketplace, with market discipline, or Adam Smith's so-called Invisible Hand, keeping costs down and quality up. So why was it necessary to organize hundreds, or thousands, of people in large organizations? Why hire them, in other words, instead of simply contracting with them in the open market?

Coase concluded that corporations were necessary because of what he called transaction costs. It might be just as cheap or cheaper to hire labor as needed in the marketplace. But that calculation ignored the difficulty of searching for and finding the right worker at the right moment, the time and cost of bargaining for a price, the need to protect trade secrets, the need to communicate with workers, and other costs. Companies found it easier to avoid these costs of dealing with the marketplace by producing what they needed internally.

But today technology has reduced many of those transaction costs. Finding the right person at the right time with the right experience is easier than it has ever been, thanks to the Internet. The costs of bargaining are also reduced, and the ability of people to communicate and collaborate with one another is enhanced by technology as well.

As these transaction costs decline, is it possible that the justification for large firms and traditional management will cease to exist?

There's a small but influential group of thinkers who argue that has already begun to happen. They point to things like Linux, a computer operating system that is built and maintained collaboratively by independent engineers all over the world, or Wikipedia, the encyclopedia maintained online by millions of users, as examples of the new model for a potentially organization-free world.

In their book *Wikinomics*, Don Tapscott and Anthony Williams cite the coming of "mass collaboration," allowing employees, consumers, community members, and taxpayers to have the power to innovate and create value on the global stage. They predict we could be at the birth "of a new era, perhaps even a golden one, on par with the Italian renaissance or the rise of Athenian democracy. Mass collaboration across borders, disciplines, and cultures is at once economical and enjoyable. . . . A new economic democracy is emerging in which we all have a lead role."

I'm particularly familiar with these arguments because they've recently infiltrated the journalism business. Pundits like Jeff Jarvis, a successful blogger who teaches college journalism courses, is unmoved by the collapse of big city newspapers and argues "citizen journalists" will arise to take their place. In short, anyone with a PDA will be able to write about, photograph, and take video of news events, and publish it online through services like Flickr and Twitter, where others can consume it. The writer and the reader will become the same. The "prosumer," as Tapscott and Williams call these thoroughly modern minions who both produce and consume, will become the new unit of industry.

I have no crystal ball, but I remain somewhat skeptical.

For one thing, no one has yet figured out how these Linux engineers and Wikipedia contributors and citizen journalists are going to earn a living. Right now, they do what they do as a labor of love. But if this is going to become the way of all commerce, then it will have to provide people with the means to feed and house a family. We may find that while some of Coase's transactions costs—the cost of searching for people with the right talents, for instance—are clearly reduced by technology, other transaction costs may actually be increased, as increasing complexity calls for a degree of coordination and quality control that "mass collaboration" can't provide.

Still, while the utopian end of mass collaboration may be in question, the benefits to be gained from tapping the expertise of a global community are not. The principles of Wikinomics—openness, networks of peers, widely shared information—can be critical building blocks in constructing a strategy for managing change.

Another prominent management guru of our times, Gary Hamel, doesn't call for the dissolution of corporations, but he does argue that the rapid pace of change calls for a radically new approach to management. In his book *The Future of Management*, Hamel argues that management has simply failed to keep up with the pace of innovation around us. "Like the combustion engine," he writes, management "is a technology that has largely stopped evolving, and that's not good."

Hamel doesn't attempt to spell out in detail what the new management order should look like. But he says it has to make companies more adaptable than they are today. In the current management paradigm:

> Deep change is nearly always crisis-led, episodic, and programmatic—accomplished through a top-to-bottom cascade of tightly scripted messages, events, goals, and actions. Sadly, it is rarely opportunity-led, continuous, and a product of the organization's intrinsic capacity to learn and adapt. While one can celebrate Lou Gerstner's turnaround at IBM, Carlos Ghosn's Lazarus-like resurrection of Nissan, or Rosemary Bravo's revitalization of the Burberry fashion brand, a turnaround is transformation tragically delayed—an expensive substitute for well-timed adaptation.

The goal, he argues, is to build organizations that are capable of continual, trauma-free renewal. And that may require some fundamentally new principles for management. Among the possible changes:

- **Efficiency** was the goal of the old school of management. But the efficient organization may squeeze out the time and resources necessary for serendipitous exploration and discovery. That's why Google, for instance, lets its workers spend up to 20 percent of their time working on projects unrelated to the company's core business. Like good venture capitalists, Google's managers know that for every 1,000 oddball ideas, there will be only about 100 worth experimenting with, only about 10 worth investing in; and only one or two that will ultimately produce a business bonanza. Finding the one or two is not an efficient process.
- **Capital allocation** is the central function of the large

corporation. But centralized capital allocation, based on projected rates of return, may overlook new technologies that have the potential to disrupt the business in the future. To encourage serendipitous discovery of the sort discussed above, organizations must find a way to invest like venture capitalists.

- **Hierarchical structures** are still the essence of today's large organizations. Most people still have a "boss" of some sort, who reports up to another "boss," and so on. But ever-shifting teams of peers may be what is needed for the future. Hamel writes about creating a company "where the spirit of community, rather than the machinery of bureaucracy, binds people together."

- **Research and development** is often a separate department in most firms. But in the future, every single employee may need to be enlisted in the overarching goal of continuous innovation and given the tools and freedom to do so.

CHANGE in Brief

- Organizations faced with disruptive change find traditional "good management" techniques may cause them to miss a big shift in their business.

- If you think you've spotted an innovation that could be disruptive to your business, you may need to devote resources to it, even if they aren't justified by expected return on investment.

- Before driving major change in an organization, you need to create a sense of urgency that change is needed.

- The organization of the future may need to be even less efficient, less hierarchical, and engage every employee in continuous innovation.

Further Reading

The Innovator's Dilemma, by Clayton Christensen, Collins, 1997. In one of the most important business books of our times, Christensen shows why so many companies fail to adapt in the face of technological change.

Leading Change, by John P. Kotter, Harvard Business Press, 1996. Kotter provides a very practical guide to instituting change at large organizations.

Who Says Elephants Can't Dance, by Louis Gerstner, HarperCollins, 2002. The inside story of one of the greatest business transformations of modern times, at IBM.

Game-Changer, by A.G. Lafley and Ram Charan, Crown Business, 2008. Worth reading because of Lafley's inspirational management style.

Wikinomics, by Dan Tapscott and Anthony D. Williams, Portfolio, 2006. If you believe in fairy tales, you may find this a compelling one. Even if you don't, the book raises some important and provocative questions about the future.

The Future of Management, by Gary Hamel with Bill Breen, Harvard Business Press, 2007. Hamel is one of the most creative management thinkers of our times, and this book is his call for a radical rethink of basic management practices.

As companies get larger, you find more and more of the enterprise is devoted to the maintenance of things we've already done and their extension, as opposed to the creation of new activities. . . . We made a decision more then fifteen years ago to fund basic research in computer science in addition to our normal development activities. By doing that across the company, we've been able to prepare ourselves for the inevitable changes that come.

CRAIG MUNDIE, *director of research, Microsoft,*
in a video interview for The Wall Street Journal's
Lessons in Leadership series

Chapter NINE

FINANCIAL LITERACY

Don't skip this chapter.

This book is about managing people. It's about harnessing a group of human beings to a common goal, and driving them to succeed.

But doing that requires resources. Money. And to be successful as a manager, you have to understand the basic tools for managing money. It's not enough for you to say "Oh, I'll leave that to the finance department," or, "I'll hire a finance person to handle that." If you don't master the fundamentals of finance, you'll wake up one day and find they have mastered you.

If you think I'm exaggerating, consider the case of WorldCom, which perpetrated the largest accounting fraud in U.S. history.

WorldCom was a high-flying telecommunications company in the late 1990s, which provided long-distance services but also provided much of the backbone for the Internet. Its chief financial officer was a man named Scott Sullivan, who—before the scandal—got high marks on Wall Street. "Scott was well regarded as a straight shooter who had his arms around a lot of the details," a Lehman Brothers analyst told my *Wall Street Journal* colleagues Shawn Young and Evan Perez.

Beginning in 1999, however, WorldCom's fortunes took a downturn.

To prevent the company from reporting huge losses, Sullivan adopted some internal accounting changes. In particular, the company was paying billions of dollars each year to local telephone companies for carrying its long-distance calls—charges known as "line costs." Sullivan simply recategorized many of those charges from an "expense" to a "capital expenditure"—allowing him to spread them out over future years and minimize short-term losses.

It was a breathtakingly simple change. And it was utterly inappropriate—accounting rules are clear that "capital expenditures" have to be tied to long-lasting investments, like, say, a new factory.

Amazingly, the fraud went on for nearly *two years* before anyone noticed! Finally, in the spring of 2002, an internal auditor named Cynthia Cooper alerted the board that something was amiss, triggering a spate of investigations that ultimately found WorldCom had overstated earnings by some *$11 billion.*

In the case of WorldCom, courts found that CEO Bernie Ebbers knew about and was complicit in Sullivan's fraud. Yet it was clear many others inside and outside the company, who should have known better, never caught on.

You didn't have to have years of accounting training to understand that what Sullivan was doing was wrong. All you needed were the basics. And that's what we'll try to teach you in this chapter.

The emphasis here won't be on how to prepare detailed financial reports. Rather, we'll focus on how to understand them, and how to use them to your advantage as a manager. Throughout the chapter, we'll be guided by this piece of wisdom from former Baruch College business professor Aaron Levenstein:

Statistics are like a bikini. What they reveal is interesting. But what they hide is vital.

BUDGETS

Budgets are an inescapable part of the management process. They are useful in planning future activities, coordinating activities among departments, communicating plans in a concrete way to everyone in the organization, and monitoring progress.

In many organizations, they are also used to evaluate performance. "Did you make budget?" is often the first question asked at performance review time.

That's a mistake. Our advice is that you should use budgets for planning, coordinating, communicating, and monitoring, but *not* for evaluating performance. Evaluating performance against budgets leads to endless internal game playing that will keep you and your team from performing at its best.

Think about what happens at budget time. A call goes out to every department to estimate expenses and/or income for the coming year. And then the game begins.

If you are in sales, and you know your performance and pay are going to be based on how well you do against your budget, there will be an enormous temptation to minimize sales projections. This is going to be a tough year for sales, you'll argue. Strong headwinds are working against you. Better keep projections low, so you can exceed expectations.

If you run the technology department, on the other hand, you'll be tempted to overstate your needs. A lot of big projects coming down the pipeline, you'll say, and we're going to need the resources to deal with them.

Meantime, the folks in the front office preparing for the budget review have the exact opposite set of incentives. They're more likely compensated on growth in the business, so they'll want to set sales projections high and keep expenses low in order to shoot for maximum profit.

The result is an intricate internal dance—a negotiation, really—that results in a budget compromise. The sales department projects 4 percent growth, the front office wants 8 percent, and the final budget settles on 6 percent. Knowing that's how the negotiation usually plays out, the parties may exaggerate their opening bids—sales says 3 percent, the front office asks for 9 percent.

You get the picture. The whole exercise wastes time and discourages candor. Moreover, the process works against risky, high-reward growth projects. If the risks are high, there'll be a strong temptation to understate the potential rewards in order to keep expectations low. There's little encouragement to think big.

Instead of budget-based compensation, we'd recommend a system in which bonuses are based not on internally negotiated numbers, but on real-world comparisons. How has the business performed compared to last year? How is it doing compared to the competition? This minimizes the game playing and gets everyone focused on the same goals.

Preparing an operating budget for most businesses involves a five-step process, as follows:

1. **Project your expected revenues.** This is often the least reliable number in your budget, particularly if you are talking about a new business. But it's important you come up with numbers grounded in experience.
2. **Calculate the expected costs of the goods sold.** This number focuses on the direct costs of your product—such as salaries and materials.
3. **Calculate other expected costs.** This is where you include things like R&D, design, marketing, administration.

4. **Calculate the expected operating income**—that is, number 1 minus number 2 and number 3.

5. **Develop alternative scenarios.** This one is critical. There's a lot of guesswork that goes into creating an operating budget. What if your guesses are wrong? It's important to develop alternative scenarios so you have a sense of the full range of possible outcomes.

THE BALANCE SHEET

The balance sheet is the foundation of accounting. It is intended to be a snapshot of the organization's **assets** and **liabilities** at a given time. Since many of the numbers in it are historical, the balance sheet may seem to be an arcane document that hides more than it reveals. But it's still important to understand the concepts that underpin balance sheet accounting in order to fully understand the income and cash statements we'll be talking about later.

In standard accounting, the balance sheet has two sides. The left-hand side is a list of all the **assets** of the organization. The right-hand side is a list of **liabilities** plus **shareholder equity**. By definition, the left-hand side and the right-hand side are always in "balance"—that is, **assets = liabilities + shareholders equity.**

Below is a sample balance sheet for an imaginary company that manufactures unicycles.

EUNICE'S UNIQUE UNICYCLES
(in thousands of dollars)

Assets

Cash and marketable securities	75
Accounts receivable	35

Inventory	20
Prepaid Expenses	12
Total current assets	142
Gross property plant equipment	2100
Less accumulated depreciation	750
Net property plant equipment	1350
Total assets	1492

Liabilities and Owner's Equity

Accounts payable	42
Accrued expenses	10
Income tax payable	15
Short-term debt	205
Total current liabilities	272
Long-term debt	200
Total liabilities	472
Contributed capital	800
Retained earnings	220
Total owner's equity	1020
Liabilities & owner's equity	1492

Total Assets. The first assets listed on the balance sheet are known as **current assets,** which includes cash as well as any asset that, in the normal course of business, is likely to be turned into cash in a year's time. That includes **marketable securities, accounts receivable** (payments due the company) minus an **allowance for doubtful accounts** (payments unlikely to be made), **inventories,** and **prepaid expenses.**

Assets also includes plant and equipment, also known as **fixed assets.** The general practice is to carry these assets on the balance sheet at their historical cost (even though replacing them may cost more), and to subtract a certain amount for **depreciation** each year, based on the plant or equipment's **estimated useful life.**

In addition, the organization may have **other assets,** including intangibles such as **patents,** which also reduce in value each year through a process of **amortization.** Then there is a catchall category of intangible assets known as **goodwill,** which often comes into play when a company is bought at a price that is far above the value of the assets on its balance sheet.

Liabilities. Again, the balance sheet starts with **current liabilities**—things likely to be paid within the next twelve months. It includes **accounts payable**—bills owed, but not yet paid, and **accrued expenses**—goods or services consumed, but not yet paid for—and **income taxes payable** but not yet paid.

Long-term liabilities can include deferred income taxes as well as long-term debt.

Shareholder Equity. In accounting theory, the excess of assets over liabilities belongs to the shareholders. In theory, this is the firm's net worth—although because of historical accounting conventions, it may have little relationship to the organization's market value.

The accounting conventions for shareholder equity are somewhat byzantine. Common and preferred stock is generally carried on the balance sheet at "par" value—rather than its current market value. Amounts paid by shareholders to the company in excess of par value are carried on the books as **additional paid-in capital.** Shareholders' equity also includes **earnings retained** by the company, **foreign currency adjustments,** and **unrealized gains on available-for-sale securities.**

The end result is a **Total Shareholders Equity** number that has very little meaning to anyone in the real world.

Still, there is useful information for managers in the balance sheet. One important measure, for instance, is **working capital**—which is calculated by subtracting current liabilities from current assets. In general, you'd like to see a healthy cushion there to assure you can deal with unexpected occurrences. Some managers and investors calculate a **current ratio** by dividing current assets by current liabilities.

Another number to keep an eye on is **quick assets**. Current assets include inventories, which may not always be easy to sell, as well as prepaid expenses, which usually can't be converted back into cash. Subtract those two from current assets and you'll get quick assets. Subtract current liabilities from quick assets and you'll get **net quick assets**. Keeping all these measures in positive territory is important for the organization's health.

Notice that on all these measures, Eunice is headed for trouble!

INCOME STATEMENTS

The income statement is the most important financial statement you'll deal with.

As discussed above, the budget is an effort to plan where your organization is going financially. The income statement is an effort to show where it actually has been.

The basic equation for the income statement is the same as for the operating budget. You start with revenues, you subtract costs, and the result is profits.

But budgets are usually internal documents, and budget conventions vary widely from organization to organization. Income statements, on the other hand, are more public documents. They are often subject to audits, they generally follow established accounting procedures, and as a result they tend to be more complicated.

For example, below is Eunice's income statement:

EUNICE'S UNIQUE UNICYCLES

(in thousands of dollars)

Net Sales	1,150
Cost of sales	785
Gross margin	365
Operating Expenses	
Depreciation and amortization	35
Selling, general and administrative expenses	112
Total Operating Expenses	147
Operating income	218
Other income	5
Total income	223
Interest expense	42
Income before income taxes	181
Income taxes	37
Net income	144

Net Sales. The first line usually reflects the organization's most important source of revenue. It's called "net" sales because it makes allowance for goods that are returned or sold at discount prices.

Cost of Sales. This represents all the costs of the organization that are identified with the purchase and manufacture of the unicycles, including materials, labor, and manufacturing overhead.

Gross Margin. The excess of sales over the cost of sales. Divide gross margin by net sales to calculate the **gross margin percentage.**

Depreciation and Amortization. This represents the decline in value of plants, equipment, and other long-lived assets, including intangibles such as a patent.

Selling, General, and Administrative Expenses. These include advertising, promotion, sales agents' salaries and commissions, travel and entertainment, executive salaries, office expenses, etc.

Operating Income. Subtract selling, general and administrative expenses, and depreciation and amortization from the gross margin to get this number.

Dividend and Interest Income. This is revenue from financial investments and is therefore counted separately from the income of the **business.**

Interest Expense. Interest paid to bondholders is a fixed charge and can be deducted from operating income before determining taxes.

Income Taxes. Taxes paid, after accounting for tax credits, etc.

Net Income. This is the bottom line—what the organization made after accounting for its expenses, overhead, depreciation, interest on debt, and taxes.

Analyzing income statements is most useful if you can compare years. For instance, you can calculate the organization's **operating margin** by dividing operating income by net sales. The number itself may tell you relatively little, since different organizations have widely different operating margins. A successful software firm could have operating margins approaching 50 percent, while a retail operation may have an operating margin of only 2 or 3 percent. But you should compare your operating margins to others in the same industry, and compare it to other years. A sharp drop in margins is a cause for some careful investigation.

Net profit ratio is another way of analyzing performance over time, similar to the operating margin, calculated by dividing net income by net sales.

For public companies, the income statement will include some extra lines that calculate **earnings per share**, a number your investors will keep a close eye on.

STATEMENT OF CASH FLOWS

Income statements are calculated using the accrual method of accounting. What that means is that transactions are recognized when, according to a bunch of complicated accounting rules, the "earnings process is completed."

What it *doesn't* mean is that cash related to those transactions has necessarily either come in or gone out of your bank account. Cash from certain merchandise sales may not come in until long after the product has been delivered, and thus been recognized on the income statement. Other transactions may be paid for in advance but not recognized on the income statement until they occur. In other words, once again, what the income statement reveals is interesting, but what it hides is vital.

A statement of cash flows can help you get your hands around the actual cash position of your organization. There are three categories, or types of cash flows in most organizations—cash from operations, cash from sale or purchase of assets, and cash from financing activities. The cash statement deals with all three. Here's a look at Eunice's cash flows for the period above (again, in thousands of dollars):

Net income	144

Operating Assets and Liabilities

Accounts receivable	(35)
Finished goods inventory	(20)
Prepaid expenses	(12)
Accounts payable	42
Accrued expenses	10
Income tax payable	(15)

Depreciation expense	<u>7</u>
Total changes in operating assets and liabilities	<u>(23)</u>
Cash flow from operations	121

Investing Activities

Sale of property, plant & equip.	11
Capital expenditures	<u>(55)</u>
Cash flow from investing	(44)

Financing Activities

Short-term debt increase	20
Long-term borrowing	10
Capital stock	0
Cash dividends to stockholders	<u>(40)</u>
Cash from financing	<u>(10)</u>
Increase in cash during year	67

Accounts Receivable. These represent unicycles that Eunice built and delivered during the year but hasn't received payment for yet.

Finished Goods Inventory. These are unicycles that were built but not yet sold.

Prepaid Expenses. These are expenses that were paid by the company for products or services not yet consumed. Accounts receivable, finished goods, and prepaid expenses are all assets for the organization that boost its accounting income, but they provide no cash.

Accounts Payable. These are goods or services you received during the year but that you haven't yet paid for.

Accrued Expenses. These are also expenses that represent items received but not paid for. **Accounts payable** and **accrued expenses**

are subtracted when calculating **net income** but are added back for purposes of calculating **cash flow**.

The difference between **income taxes** owed for activities during the year and those actually paid during the year can also affect your cash balance, as can **depreciation**, which is subtracted on your income statement but doesn't represent a cash expense.

Investment Activities. If you either sell or buy capital assets, that will likely affect your cash flow.

Financing Activities. Borrowing obviously brings in cash, as do additional stock sales. Cash dividends paid to shareholders, on the other hand, reduce your cash flow. (Note that interest payments on your debt are already accounted for in net income. Dividends are not, since they are generally not mandatory.)

The cash flow statement can be an important source of information about what's going on in the organization. If net income is growing faster than cash from operations, for instance, that could be a warning signal that something is going awry. Eunice may be making more unicycles than the market can support (thus building up inventories), or selling them to people who are unlikely to pay (thus boosting accounts receivable.)

CONSTRUCT A FINANCIAL DASHBOARD

Financial statements offer a wealth of information—often more than you can readily monitor. Depending on the nature of your organization, you'll probably want to find a few key financial measurements that you can monitor on a regular basis.

We've mentioned some of the possibilities in the sections above. Most businesses want to keep a close eye on their **operating margins** as a basic sign of health. And if you're worried about the short-term viability of your organization, you may also want to watch the **current ratio** or **net quick assets** figures very closely.

The **asset turnover ratio** is a way of looking at how well the company's assets are being employed to generate sales revenue. It's calculated by dividing sales by total assets. The ratio varies from industry to industry, but the higher the turnover rate, the better.

How leveraged is your organization? It's worth looking at how big a percentage of **operating income** is used up by **interest expense,** and tracking that over time. Another way of monitoring debt is to add together your income plus interest plus taxes, and then divide by interest expense to find out how much of your income is being eaten up by debt payments.

There are endless variations here. You may also want to monitor how quickly your accounts receivable are being paid, or how rapidly inventories are turning over. Which measures you watch will depend on your organization's particular goals and vulnerabilities. It's worth the time to figure out some of those measurements, and be disciplined in tracking them regularly.

TIME VALUE OF MONEY

Suppose you buy a house for $500,000 and sell it for $750,000. What's your return on investment? That's simple, right? It's $250,000, or 50 percent. Not bad.

But there's a critical piece of information missing from that ROI calculation. How long did you own the house? If you only owned it for a year, then you deserve the investor of the year award. But if you owned it for thirty years, you may wonder why it increased so little in value.

The basic point here is that a dollar today is worth more than a dollar next year. How much more depends on the opportunities you have to invest that dollar. In the simplest example, if a bank will pay you 4 percent on your cash deposits, then $100 today is worth at least $104 a year from now.

So when you calculate your return on an investment, it's not good enough to figure out how much money you earn in the future. You have to calculate the **present value** of that return.

We're not going to give you a mathematical lesson in calculating present values here. The good news is there are plenty of calculators readily available to do the job for you. But we aren't going to let you leave this chapter without understanding how these calculations are made.

Let's start with a simple example. You invest $100,000 in a piece of property that you expect eventually to sell for $150,000. What's the **present value** of that future sale?

That depends on two things. One is how long it will take you to make the sale. The other is the "discount rate" for the investment. This can vary from person to person or company to company, but basically it's the cost of money. If you paid 6 percent interest a year to borrow the money, then that's the discount rate you should use. If you took money out of your savings account that pays you 4 percent a year, then that's your discount rate.

We'll spare you the mathematics, but if your discount rate is 4 percent and you make your sale in five years, the present value is $123,300, so you made, in present value terms, $23,300. If your discount rate is 6 percent and you don't sell for ten years, the present value is only $83,700. Assuming you borrowed the money, you would have been better off not doing the deal.

A variation on the theme is **net present value**, which is the present value of the future cash flows from an investment, *minus* the initial investment. Needless to say, if you project a **net present value** that's negative, you shouldn't make the investment. If it's positive, then you need to match it against the **net present value** of alternative investment schemes.

These calculations can get complicated pretty quickly. For instance, in most investments, the return won't all come the same year. Thus you have to discount cash flows for each year. Likewise, your investment probably won't be made all up front, so you need to apply the discount rate to the stream of investment spending as well, since a dollar invested next year is less costly than a dollar invested today.

And, of course, keep in mind these calculations are only as good as the assumptions underlying them. It's not always easy to know, for instance, what your discount rate should be. If you are borrowing the money, you could find interest rates swing wildly over the investment period. Your estimates of future cash flows will probably be even more uncertain. It's best to calculate alternative scenarios, so you fully understand the possible outcomes and aren't slave to one calculation.

One last concept you need to get your head around is **internal rate of return.** That's a popular concept used in business to measure an investment. Again, we're not going to teach you how to make the calculation on your own. But the concept is fairly simple. We've already talked about calculating an investment's **net present value** using a particular discount rate. The **internal rate of return** is simply the discount rate you would need to use in that calculation to make the net present value equal to zero. Thus, the **internal rate of return** on any investment with positive **net present value** will be greater than the **discount rate.**

Thoroughly confused? Want to learn more? As always, we offer some suggestions for further reading. The first is a workbook I was forced to navigate before attending the Senior Executive Program at the Stanford Graduate School of Business. I recommend it highly.

FINANCIAL LITERACY in Brief

- If you don't master the fundamentals of finance, they will master you.
- Don't evaluate your team by comparing their results to budget. Compare results to the real world.
- Construct a personal dashboard of financial measures you want to keep a close eye on. One suggestion: the current ratio, which is current assets divided by current liabilities. If it falls below one, watch out!

Further Reading

Essentials of Accounting, by Leslie K. Breitner and Robert N. Anthony, Prentice Hall, 1997. This is basically a workbook that will teach you the essential concepts in a clear and coherent way.

Manager's Toolkit, by Harvard Business Press, 2004. A useful primer for managers, with a good section on financial tools.

We identify leaders very early on. And once we have identified them, we expose them to different parts of the world. There is nobody at the general management level who has not been working at least in three, four, five different countries in the world.

PETER BRABECK-LEMATHE, *chairman, Nestlé,*
in a video interview for The Wall Street Journal's
Lessons in Leadership series

Chapter TEN

GOING GLOBAL

The financial crisis of 2008 likely marked a turning point in the history of global business.

From the end of World War II, American companies, buoyed by the irrepressible American consumer and fueled by the world's most robust financial system, dominated the globe. The United States alone accounted for a quarter of the world's economic output.

But in 2008, the U.S. financial system collapsed, with storied institutions like Lehman Brothers and Merrill Lynch disappearing as independent entities, while others, like Citigroup and Bank of America, fell into the arms of the U.S. government. Consumers, overextended with mountains of debt backed by once-inflated housing values, were forced to put away their wallets and begin slowly paying down debts. To be sure, the crisis hit the rest of the world as hard, or harder, than the United States. But neither the American financial system nor the American consumer seemed likely to regain their central role in the global economic equation for many years to come.

Meanwhile, the Chinese government emerged from the crisis in surprisingly robust shape. Enormous Chinese surpluses of foreign cash became the bank that the U.S. government had to tap to finance swelling budget deficits. And while U.S. government stimulus measures were mired in bureaucratic muck, the Chinese proved remarkably adept at using centralized power to stoke a new round of economic growth.

History, of course, can take surprising turns, and the story of American decline has been foretold—falsely—before. But it's hard to look at recent events without feeling that the torch may have been passed.

What will that new global era mean for managers? Well, to get a taste, it's worth looking at the lives of two men who have already entered it—Carlos Ghosn, the CEO of Renault Group of France and Nissan Motor Company of Japan, and Howard Stringer, the first foreign CEO of Sony Corporation.

Ghosn is a walking symbol of globalization. He is a Frenchman, born in Brazil of Lebanese parents. He is fluent in four languages— English, French, Portuguese, and Arabic. And the companies he oversees operate in more than a hundred countries of the world. He spends much of his life on an airplane, touching down in various locations, and working to leave a strong imprint of his management style everywhere he visits. His Paris office has three clocks—one each displaying the time in Paris, Tokyo, and Nashville, Tennessee.

The *Journal*'s Monica Langley accompanied him on one of his globe-trotting trips in 2006, when he visited a Renault plant in Maubeuge, France, delivering his message about the carmaker's commitment to boost profit margins by 50 percent over the next three years.

"*Commitment* is a strong word," one manager challenged him, "and circumstances have changed" since the goal was set earlier that year.

"It's not a target," Mr. Ghosn snapped back. "Either management performs or it's out . . . and that applies to me as well."

Mr. Ghosn's abrupt, no-excuses attitude may seem harsh, but for a man who has to oversee such a large global company, operating in so many different languages and cultures over such vast geography, subtlety is not an option. He is known as something of a micromanager, weighing in not just on car designs and advertising campaigns, but also even on the wording of management brochures and the cleanliness of factory floors. Since he can't be everywhere at once, he makes his presence felt where and when he is, even selecting the music to be played at his public appearances.

At the French plant, which makes compact vans, Ghosn bores in on a high absenteeism rate. "We have a 4 percent rate," he chastises the factory's top managers; "Peugeot and Toyota factories nearby have 2 percent. . . . Does your action plan include getting rid of those not playing by the rules? An absent employee penalizes his team. With 14 percent unemployment in this area, I want those who really want to work."

Like Ghosn, Stringer is himself something of a global melting pot, born in Wales, but a naturalized citizen of the United States and a veteran of the Vietnam War. He cut his teeth running the CBS television network before becoming the first non-Japanese CEO of Sony Corporation in 2005.

Stringer hopped back and forth between Tokyo and New York, and soon found himself under attack in both places—but for very different reasons. Japanese financial analysts and Sony employees slammed him for living in a hotel and being disconnected from the company's daily operations, while U.S. investors criticized him for not moving faster to fix Sony's problems.

"Look," a clearly annoyed Stringer told Yukari Kane and Phred Dvorak of the *Journal* in a 2007 interview in Tokyo, "in America, I was told to cut costs. In Japan, I was told not to cut costs. Two different worlds. In this country, you can't lay people off very easily. In America, you can."

With the once iconic electronics company lagging in comparison to competitors like Apple, Stringer felt the pressure to act quickly. But at the same time, he recognized there was much in Sony culture worth respecting and preserving. "I don't want to change Sony's culture to the point where it's unrecognizable from the founder's vision," he said.

"That's the balancing act I'm doing. . . . You can't go through a Japanese company with a sledgehammer."

The cultural balancing act caused him to gain a reputation as a "hands-off" manager, and to move slowly in dealing with some obvious problems. One such problem was Ken Kutaragi, head of Sony's video games division and inventor of the PlayStation video game consoles. Kutaragi cultivated a reputation as a renegade, refusing to communicate with other Sony units or even his own bosses. In 2005, he hosted an event at a big electronics conference in Las Vegas to celebrate the launch of the PlayStation Portable handheld game machine, and didn't invite executives from Sony's electronics division, which provided the parts.

Stringer initially tried to win Kutaragi's cooperation with patience. "I've had dinner with [Kutaragi] more times than I've had dinner with my wife, and that's not really healthy," he told the *Journal*.

Eventually, Stringer's patience ran out. He took Kutaragi out from running day-to-day operations in 2006, and the Japanese executive resigned from Sony in 2007.

Others have found globalization even more difficult. Jürgen Schrempp, CEO of German automaker Daimler, launched a global expansion in the late 1990s that involved a $36 billion merger with Chrysler, as well as buying a stake in Japan's Mitsubishi Motors and forging an alliance with Korea's Hyundai Motors.

Schrempp's empire building fell apart, piece by piece. Daimler unwound its investment in Mitsubishi in 2004 following mounting losses, and ended its alliance with Hyundai the same year. Then in 2007, with the U.S. auto industry foundering, the German company effectively gave away its interest in Chrysler to private equity firm Cerberus.

More recently, the Japanese brokerage firm Nomura Holdings Inc. has struggled to assimilate the businesses it bought from the bankrupt Lehman Brothers. The process has been particularly tough for women. The *Journal*'s Alison Tudor reported in 2009 that a group of Harvard grads hired by Lehman before it collapsed found themselves in Nomura training sessions where they were taught how to wear their hair, how to serve tea, and how to choose their wardrobe according to the season.

"Nomura is more internationally minded than its Japanese banking peers," a former Nomura banker told the *Journal*, "but there is still a gulf between it and Western investment banks."

MANAGING IN A GLOBAL WORLD

So what's a manager to conclude from these cautionary tales? First, that the global business world is an inescapable reality of modern existence. And odds are, it's likely to be a central part of your experience as a manager.

That has very real implications for how you do your job. Among them:

You must learn to manage from afar. Once upon a time, most managers had their workers nearby, and management was a contact sport. But today there's a good chance you'll find some of your workers aren't nearby, and may be thousands of miles away. You may have to manage outsourcing or other relationships with groups overseas, and you may be working with people who don't speak your language, or speak it imperfectly.

That only increases the importance of having a very clear set of goals, agreed to and committed to by all parties, and an agreed upon set of measurements for achieving those goals.

When you're in close contact with your team and share a common language and culture, you might be able to afford a little ambiguity. When they are on the other side of the globe, you can't.

You must learn to be respectful of other traditions and cultures. This becomes another strong argument for diversity. You can use people on your team who speak multiple languages, have worked in different places and understand different cultures to help you navigate the shoals. You've got to be sensitive to cultural differences—but at the same time, you can't let that "sensitivity" get in the way of clear and candid communication, goal setting, and accountability.

If you're smart, you'll look for opportunities to travel abroad yourself and expand your own horizons. You may even want to take up a foreign language. It can only help prepare you for the world ahead.

Your strategic plan must take into account developments overseas. Just because you've never been subject to competition from overseas in the past doesn't mean you won't be in the future. The world is shrinking, and competition is playing out on a global stage. You have to keep a close eye on potential overseas competition, as well as on potential overseas suppliers.

Take care before starting a venture overseas. "Go global!" sometimes seems like a business imperative these days—much like "Go West!" was in the nineteenth century. But our advice is to proceed with caution. There's a temptation to take the Schrempp approach and dive headlong without fully analyzing the hidden costs and the unforeseen consequences. Best to explore those more fully in advance by asking and answering the following three questions:

1. **What are the benefits of the proposed move overseas?** Is it primarily to reduce costs—by, for instance, taking advantage of lower-cost outsourcing? Is it to expand the market for your goods and services, because the domestic market is mature or stagnant? Or is it to acquire critical knowledge or experience that will be necessary to the organization's ability to survive and thrive?

2. **Does your organization have the capabilities for this expansion?** Do you have established relationships in the market you are moving into? Do you have people willing to do extensive travel or who have the necessary language skills to oversee the business and maintain the relationships? Are you, as manager, willing to take on the responsibility of overseeing an international operation, which inevitably will require more of your time and attention than an expansion of the same size domestically will require?

3. **Don't make the mistake of thinking you can simply appoint a deputy to oversee the international operation.** Expanding into other countries is a strategic decision, and if it is to be successful, it needs to be overseen by top management.

4. **Do the benefits outweigh the costs? This is where organizations usually go wrong.** That's because it's easy to calculate the savings of, say, a decision to outsource tech services to India, but much harder to calculate the unforeseen costs—the frustration and wasted time of customers and employees who have to deal with tech support workers who don't seem to know the first thing about your business. It's worth spending time exploring these potential costs, and then trying to match them up with the benefits.

If it's a close call, don't do it—as the odds are high you've overlooked some of the costs. Don't let the "Go global" imperative trick you into doing something stupid. As we'll discuss in the next section, the world isn't yet as flat as some would have you believe.

THE LIMITS OF GLOBALIZATION

New York Times columnist Thomas L. Friedman captured the imagination of a world trying to understand rapid globalization with his book *The World Is Flat*. It made for a great cover photo—with giant, Columbus-era sailing ships about to fall off the edge of the world.

But while the world may be *flatter* than it was, the truth is, it's still far from flat. As business scholar Pankaj Ghemawat shows in his book, *Redefining Global Strategy*, differences among nations still matter a great deal in modern business, and will continue to matter for the foreseeable future.

A few facts make the point. Consider that foreign direct investment—that is, investment by companies outside of their country of origin—remains less than 10 percent of all investment. Or to put it another way, 90 percent of all the investments that companies do make happens within the countries in which they are located.

Telephone traffic is even more localized—less than 5 percent of all the minutes spent on phone calls are across international boundaries. Even U.S. stock investments, which can easily jump borders, remain roughly 85 percent in U.S. companies.

Ghemawat traces Coca-Cola's efforts to deal with globalization in recent decades as a cautionary tale. In the 1980s Robert Goizueta rapidly expanded overseas in the belief that Coke's market share should be the same all over the world. He created a highly centralized system to sell a standardized product in every country in the world.

But soon after he died in 1997, it became clear that this one-size-fits-all strategy wasn't working, and the company's stock took a dive because of overseas "exposure." That left a new CEO, Douglas Daft, to declare in January 2000 that "no one drinks globally. Local people get thirsty and go to their retailer and buy a locally made Coke." He called for massive layoffs at Coke headquarters in Atlanta and launched a reorganization that put the decision making closer to the local markets. His mantra was "Think Local, Act Local." Most surprisingly, he discontinued global advertising, causing an exodus of marketing talent and sagging growth. In February 2004, the company announced his retirement.

The new CEO, Neville Isdell, made it clear that under Daft, the pendulum had "swung too far." He rebuilt some centralization at Atlanta headquarters, including global marketing, but also gave substantial power to regional managers. He has struggled to find a happy medium, recognizing the Coke brand does have global power and advantages, but also recognizing that it might not make sense to compete the same way in all markets.

In short, Coke has had to adapt to a world that is much smaller and more integrated than ever before but that is still far from flat.

The Chinese Example

The clearest evidence that business practices vary sharply around the world can be found in China, which in the last two decades has seen a spurt of economic growth unparalleled in human history.

Measured by purchasing power, China is already the world's fourth largest economy. The income of the average Chinese is still a fraction of that of the average American, but the sheer number of Chinese citizens makes up much of the difference. And when it comes to the consumption of some basic commodities, fast-growing China sets the pace—consuming, for instance, a third or more of the world's steel production.

Jim McGregor, ex-reporter, writer, and business representative for Dow Jones in China, says the country is at once the world's largest start-up and its largest turnaround. Compared to U.S. history, he writes in his book *One Billion Customers*, China:

> is undergoing the raw capitalism of the Robber Baron era of the late 1800s; the financial mania of the 1920s; the rural-to-urban migration of the 1930s; the emergence of the first-car, first-home, first-fashionable clothes, first-college education, first-family vacation, middle-class consumer of the 1950s, and even aspects of social upheaval similar to the 1960s.

The result is a land of both enormous opportunity and enormous risk. China is the world's largest consumer market and, increasingly, the world's factory. For anyone trying to run a truly global business, it is impossible to ignore. Yet it is also a place where capitalism is suffering through enormous birthing pains and still faces the overlay of a centralized, Communist government.

In 2007, a team of *Journal* reporters chronicled the birthing pains in a series of articles that won the Pulitzer Prize for Reporting. The revelations were eye-opening.

One story, for instance, explored the rampant use of poisonous lead in manufactured products. In China, that manifested itself in an isolated village in the mountains of China's western Gansu province, where nearly everyone—including hundreds of children—was found to have unsafe amounts of lead in their bodies. In the United States, it resulted in a four-year-old boy in Minneapolis dying from lead poisoning after swallowing a metal charm made in China.

Another piece looked at a village doctor who rallied farmers to take on a local chemical plant that was dumping pollutants into a nearby river. Nearly a third of China's rivers are so dirty they aren't fit even for industrial or agricultural use, and clean water has become such a problem in China that some 300 million people don't have daily access.

Here, more than anywhere in the world, managers need to enter with their eyes wide open. The siren song may be hard to resist. But it's not all sweetness.

McGregor's advice shows the unique nature of Chinese business. He writes:

- Avoid joint ventures with government entities unless you have no choice. Then understand that this partnership is about China obtaining your technology, know-how, and capital while maintaining Chinese control.
- Roll up your sleeves. There are no passive investments in China. Expect that revenue and profits will not justify the high-level management time required for the first several years.
- The Chinese appear to the West to be a collective society. They eat together, travel together, and have fun together. But always simmering just below that collective veneer is a dog-eat-dog competitive spirit that makes the Chinese among the world's most individualistic and selfish people.
- Deep scars from the Cultural Revolution and the upheaval of a sudden shift to getting rich has created an atmosphere in which nobody trusts anybody. In China's business world the expectation is that you'll be cheated.
- In China, a conflict of interest is viewed as a competitive advantage.
- If you must fight with the bureaucracy, take your fight to the highest possible level, where officials are the most reasonable and focused on China's larger interests.
- China's greatest management challenges are to create

organizations that are not dictatorships, to treat others as equals, to accept responsibility for mistakes, and to share information—all behaviors that have been almost absent.

In short, it should be clear that doing business in China is a very different thing than doing business elsewhere in the world.

GOING GLOBAL in Brief

- Today's managers must learn to manage from afar, be respectful of people from other cultures, and always consider overseas developments in formulating their strategies.
- The world isn't flat. The vast majority of today's business activity takes place within national boundaries, and even international activity is concentrated among countries in the same region or with similar cultures and traditions.
- Understanding other regions, traditions, and cultures is a valuable skill for you and your team to have.

Further Reading

One Billion Customers, by James McGregor, Wall Street Journal Books, 2005. The best guidebook available for anyone who is planning to do business in China.

The World Is Flat, by Thomas L. Friedman, Farrar, Straus and Giroux, 2005. A great read, and filled with fascinating anecdotes about the progress of globalization. But Friedman has a tendency to overstate his thesis.

Redefining Global Strategy, by Pankaj Ghemawat, Harvard Business Press, 2007. Ghemawat provides compelling evidence that the world is far from flat, and not likely to become flat anytime soon.

The Next Global Stage, by Kenichi Ohmae, Wharton School Publishing, 2005. Ohmae provides the view of global business from 10,000 feet. It's an interesting book but probably of limited practical value to those trying to figure out how to manage in this world.

When it comes to creating an ethical organization, the fundamental belief I have is that you are the role model for your organization. The old expression, "The fish stinks from the head" also has a positive connotation.

If I'm asking my folks to travel coach, then I need to model that policy myself, and not have a double standard.

RUSSELL FRADIN, *CEO, Hewitt Associates,*
in a video interview for The Wall Street Journal's
Lessons in Leadership series

Chapter **ELEVEN**

ETHICS

The first decade of the twenty-first century has taken a horrendous toll on the reputation of business.

It started with the stunning collapse of Enron Corporation, which led to the equally stunning indictment and collapse of respected accounting firm Arthur Andersen for its role in trying to cover up Enron's problems. Then came the fall of WorldCom, which improperly booked billions of dollars of expenses, and the disgrace of Citigroup analyst Jack Grubman, who touted WorldCom's fraud-fueled stock to investors around the world. Adelphia Communications Corporation founder John Rigas was charged with what the Securities and Exchange Commission called "one of the most extensive financial frauds ever to take place at a public company." And Tyco's Dennis Kozlowski and his chief financial officer were charged with looting hundreds of millions of dollars from their firm.

Kozlowski provided the iconic image of the era, in a video of an extravagant birthday party he threw, in part at company expense, for his second wife on the Italian island of Sardinia. The over-the-top soirée featured a giant ice sculpture of Michelangelo's *David* spewing vodka from its penis, a birthday cake in the shape of a woman's breasts with sparklers mounted on top, centurions in Roman garb, and near-naked young women throwing flower petals in the pool while near-naked men gyrated on pedestals. "It was a nice party," Kozlowski said at his trial, "with nice people."

The accounting scandals were followed by a steady stream of stories about excessive CEO pay practices. Pfizer Inc. CEO Hank McKinnell was chased out of office, after it was revealed that he had earned $79 million in pay and bonuses and a pension of $6 million a year for life during a period when Pfizer shareholders saw their stock value drop by almost half. Bob Nardelli was forced out of his job as CEO of Home Depot, in part because of a furor over a front-page story in the *New York Times* claiming he had earned an estimated $245 million in five years, despite Home Depot's sagging stock price. And those corporate paychecks paled in comparison to some of the giant paydays being earned by financiers during this era of excess. A few hedge fund managers such as Eddie Lampert, whose ESL Investments bought Sears and Kmart, were said to have earned more than a billion dollars in a single year.

The crowning blow to the public's view of business came with the financial crisis of 2007 to 2008. Americans had historically been tolerant of excessive, even obscene, accumulations of wealth, in part because they clung to a faith that someday, they or their children might have the opportunity to earn the same. But with the financial crisis, that faith was shattered. People saw the value of their homes and their retirement savings drop by 30 percent or 40 percent or more. And at the same time, they watched in outrage as the same financiers who had been earning outsize paychecks for the past decade paraded to Washington to collect multi-billion-dollar bailout checks, backed by the taxpayers' money, for a crisis they caused.

By the end of the decade, "business ethics" was seen by most of the public as a contradiction in terms.

WHAT IS BUSINESS ETHICS?

Peter Drucker argued that there is no such thing as "business ethics." The very phrase, he thought, suggested those in business should live by different rules than everyone else lives by.

"Executives," he wrote, "should not cheat, steal, lie, bribe, or take bribes. But nor should anyone else. Men and women do not acquire exemption from the ordinary rules of personal behavior because of their work or job."

The solution, he said, is "moral values and moral education—of the individual, of the family, of the school." He advocated stiff punishment for anyone—business executive or otherwise—who violated those rules.

But organizations do pose special ethical challenges, in part because it is not always easy to sort out the organization's legitimate interests as distinct from those of the many individuals with which it interacts—customers, suppliers, employees, etc.

Consider a simple example: a waiter at a popular restaurant offers free dessert to a table of customers who are upset about having to wait so long for their food. In return, the customers pay the waiter a big tip. Is that laudable conduct on the part of the waiter, who has turned unsatisfied customers into happy ones, and been rewarded for his success? Or has the waiter stolen from his employer, by trading off a smaller dinner check for a bigger tip?

For managers, the difficulties of distinguishing your interests from those of your organization become greater. You likely have authority to spend the organization's resources; but you have to make decisions about which expenditures are legitimate, and which aren't. Traveling to meet with a critical customer can clearly be in the interests of the organization. But what if the customer is in Paris, and you organize the visit for a Friday that coincides with a weekend when your friend is traveling to Paris as well? Are you acting in the organization's interests? Or your own?

The Tyco case was a dramatic example of an executive who lost any sense of where to draw the line. Among other things, Kozlowski kept a lavish Fifth Avenue apartment furnished with such extravagances as a $6,000 shower curtain, a $38,000 backgammon table, a $105,000 Regency mahogany bookcase, and a pair of Italian armchairs, dating back to 1780, that cost $64,000, all paid for by the company.

At his trial, Kozlowski's lawyers defended these purchases, saying the apartment was used by the CEO for business purposes. They argued that the very conspicuousness of his consumption was proof that he had done nothing wrong. There were no secret Swiss bank accounts, no cover-up attempts, none of the usual clandestine activities you'd expect from someone who was conducting a theft. The executive was so open about his conduct, they argued, that he must have believed it was a legitimate use of corporate resources and sanctioned by the board of directors.

The jury disagreed, and Kozlowski was sentenced to serve a minimum of eight years and four months in prison.

COMPANY POLICY

The extravagant mixing of business and pleasure by CEOs at company expense was illustrated in 2005 by my *Journal* colleague Mark Maremont, who cleverly matched the golf scores posted on public Internet sites operated by the USSGA and other golf associations against the flight plans of corporate aircraft, made available by commercial aviation-data services.

What he found was that the practice of CEOs using their corporate jets to fly to cushy golf resorts was astonishingly common.

On January 28 of that year, for instance, Raymond LeBoeuf of PPG Industries in Pittsburgh flew to Naples, Florida, for eighteen holes at the invitation-only Hole in the Wall club. His score was 82. The following weekend, he flew again to the Naples club, and improved his score to 77. By the time spring arrived, he had made the trip eight times.

Augusta, Georgia, home of Augusta National Golf Club, which hosts the annual Masters Tournament, was a particular favorite for the CEOs. Telephone company Alltel Corporation's four jets landed more than 165 times over four years at the Augusta airport. A company spokesman said the jets are sometimes used to travel to destinations for "customer entertainment."

Are such trips a legitimate use of the organization's resources? Many of the companies caught in Maremont's reporting net argued yes. For instance, Ed Zander, then CEO of Motorola, which is based outside of Chicago, was found to have logged ten golf scores at the exclusive Preserve Golf Club in Carmel, California, over a nine-month period. Before and after each of those games, Motorola jets flew to and from the nearby Monterey airport. The company cited a study it commissioned that concluded Zander should be required to use company jets whenever he flies, for security reasons—rather than pay for travel out of his paycheck, which was $6.1 million in 2004, plus additional stock grants valued at $9.1 million.

Companies often defend such practices by saying they are consistent with the wishes of their boards of directors, which in turn are supposed to be looking after the interests of shareholders, who ultimately own the company. LeBoeuf, for instance, said his trips to Naples were "consistent with corporate policy and the desires of the board." But it's unlikely many boards spend time watching over their CEO's golfing trips. And corporate governance experts question whether boards filled with people who may have been suggested for the job by the CEO, and who can earn $100,000 to $200,000 a year in directors' fees, are in a position to adequately oversee use of the shareholders' resources.

In 2006, Maremont, along with *Journal* reporters Charles Forelle and James Bandler, unveiled another popular corporate tactic used to line the pockets of company executives—options backdating.

Scouring corporate records, Forelle and Bandler found a large number of companies that seemed to have an uncanny ability to issue new stock options to executives when the company's stock was at a trough, ensuring big gains when the stock rose. For instance, Jeffrey Rich, CEO of Affiliated Computer Services, received his annual grant of stock options on the day that the stock price hit its lowest point in a year. Only a week later, the stock had risen 27 percent. Indeed, it turned out all of his stock-option grants from 1995 to 2002 were dated just before a steep rise in the stock price.

Was that luck? That's what Rich called it. But Forelle and Bandler calculated the odds of that favorable timing happening by chance were about one in 300 billion. Was it because the company issued the options on days when it thought the stock was about to rise? Unlikely as well, given the vagaries of the stock market. The only plausible explanation was that the option issue date was set *after the fact*, once it became clear the stock was going to rise.

Affiliated was just one of dozens of companies that showed up in Forelle and Bandler's analysis as likely backdaters. The biggest target was William McGuire, CEO of giant insurer UnitedHealth Group Inc., who held some $1.6 billion worth of company options, many of them issued at or near stock price lows. UnitedHealth had an unusual policy of letting Dr. McGuire choose the day of his own option grants. But the fortunate timing suggested he had not only picked the dates, but also had picked them after the fact.

McGuire lost his job in the scandal that followed, which caught up more than 130 companies and led to the firing or resignation of more than fifty executives and directors. "The sheer magnitude of the numbers of companies, executives and corporate boards that have disclosed options-related investigations is mind-boggling," former SEC chief accountant Lynn Turner told the *Journal*.

Yet some of the executives involved escaped unscathed, arguing they had done nothing wrong. Notable among them was Apple Computer CEO Steve Jobs, who was aware that the company had chosen favorable dates for some of its options grants. But a probe by the company's own board concluded there was no misconduct by him involved.

The options scandal represented another epidemic of cloudy ethical thinking by business. Options were originally awarded to provide workers an incentive to grow the company. But there's no incentive involved if the options have already increased in value by the time they are actually awarded.

Such a grant could be seen as just another way for the company to compensate valuable employees. But if it was just straight compensation, then why didn't the company simply pay it out in the form of salary or bonus? Was someone trying to hide the compensation from someone? Shareholders, perhaps? Or the Internal Revenue Service?

Such questions raised a complicated thicket of issues that weren't always easy to sort out. But in the end, the cases seemed to boil down to the basics of unethical behavior. There was clearly deceit involved— the company was *lying* about when the options were granted. And there was misappropriation of corporate resources involved—the money earned by grant recipients for the backdated options was in effect being *stolen* from the other shareholders.

The lessons from this decade of scandal are clear enough. Large, complex organizations offer managers ample opportunities for clouding the lines that separate what rightfully belongs to employees, shareholders, customers, suppliers, taxpayers, and so on. But at day's end, ethics still apply, and many of these complex schemes are simply *lying*, *cheating, stealing,* or *bribing,* disguised in complex garb. As a manager, you need to be constantly thinking, not about what you can get away with, but about what is right. And you need to be wary of complex schemes that lead to questionable outcomes. On matters of ethics, your gut may often be a better guide than a complicated rule book.

There's another point to keep in mind here as well. An important role of the manager is to lead by example. There is a big burden on your back. If you are fastidious about distinguishing between what rightfully belongs to the organization as opposed to you; if you don't pile on expenses that seem to benefit you more than the organization; if you don't take advantage of easy opportunities to overcharge a customer or underpay a supplier; if you don't allow anyone to play games with performance or financial metrics; then there's a much better chance that others will follow in your footsteps.

Do the opposite, and you may soon find yourself the victim of ethical lapses by others.

CREATING AN ETHICAL CULTURE

Does ethics pay?

In recent years, many business leaders have made the argument that the reason to maintain a high ethical standard is because it's good business.

Having high ethical standards, they argue, makes your customers more willing to buy from you, your employees more willing to work for you, and ultimately adds to your bottom line. As the Organization for Economic Cooperation and Development put it in a 1998 report: "Attending to legitimate social concerns should, in the long run, benefit all parties, including investors."

That's a comforting notion for those who want to believe that capitalism, at the end of the day, can cure its own ills.

But in her book *Value Shift*, Lynn Sharp Paine of the Harvard Business School argues that it's simply misleading to assume that ethical values and financial imperatives will naturally coincide. There are simply too many cases in which unethical behavior has paid off, in the short term and the long term.

As a result, ethics, she believes, has to be instituted as a separate discipline in corporations, distinct from the financial discipline. She argues compellingly that managers have to take it as a central part of their job to make sure their organization is behaving in a moral fashion.

How do you do that? As discussed above, setting the right example is critical. But beyond that, asking the right questions imposes a useful discipline. Paine argues all key decisions or actions should be subjected to a series of questions organized around four *P*s (if you haven't figured this out already, business writers love alliterative lists).

Purpose—Does this decision or action serve a worthwhile purpose? Do our goals here contribute to people's lives? And what about the means we are proposing for pursuing those goals? Do we have a sound basis for pursuing the proposed path?

Principle—Is this action consistent with relevant principles? What norms of conduct are relevant to this situation? Are we violating any of our ideals, aspirations, laws, or company codes of conduct in doing this? Are there any relevant ethical principles that need to be considered?

People—Does this action respect the legitimate claims of the people likely to be affected? Who is likely to be affected, both directly and indirectly, from the action? Who will benefit from it? Who will be injured? Will anyone's rights be violated or infringed in any way? Have we taken full advantage of the opportunities for mutual benefit?

Power—Do we have the power to take this action? What is the scope of our legitimate authority in view of relevant laws, agreements, understanding, and stakeholder expectations? Have we secured the necessary approvals or consent? Do we have the resources to carry out the action?

By instilling a discipline of asking these sorts of questions as part of your organization's decision-making process, you can help ensure you are considering the moral consequences of your actions.

CORPORATE SOCIAL RESPONSIBILITY

As shown above, the basics of organizational ethics are fairly simple: Don't lie. Don't cheat. Don't steal. And obey the laws and regulations society imposes on you.

In recent decades, however, there have been ever-rising demands on corporations to go further and engage in activities for the general benefit of society. The pressure started in the 1970s, when a group of religious and other nonprofits began pressuring companies to stop investing in South Africa, because of its apartheid policies. At around the same time, the American Jewish Congress introduced shareholder actions against companies it suspected of supporting the Arab boycott of Israel. In subsequent decades, environmental groups took the lead, pressuring companies to stop mining or drilling or logging ventures that they felt spoiled the environment.

Today corporate responsibility has become a full-fledged movement, sanctioned by the United Nations and identified by its own acronym: CSR. In Europe, in particular, many companies have adopted what's known as the "Triple Bottom Line." In theory, that means they measure their activities not only for their effect on *profit*, but also for their effect on *people* and the *planet*. The company's goal is no longer to simply benefit shareholders, but also to benefit "stakeholders"—with stakeholders defined so broadly as to include anyone whose life may be affected by the company's action.

Before he died in 2006, economist Milton Friedman was a harsh critic of this movement. The social responsibility of business, he argued vociferously, is to make a profit. Executives should be ethical, and obey the laws. But if their mission is complicated by a bunch of conflicting social mandates, they may fail. Leave it to Adam Smith's invisible hand to ensure that profit seeking adds up to broad social benefit.

Even some liberals, like economist and former labor secretary Robert Reich, have taken on the CSR movement. Reich argues that it is the job of government to pass laws to protect people and the environment, and not the job of business to do the same if government fails. Former British Labor prime minister Tony Blair echoed that point at a meeting of the World Economic Forum in Davos, when he was asked by forum organizer Klaus Schwab what responsibility business had to deal with problems like global warming. "The first responsibility of business," Blair replied, "is to run a good business."

But as Drucker points out, the modern corporation can't really escape the fact that it has many responsibilities to society. First and foremost, it must take responsibility for its own impact on society. If it is polluting the air or the water, if it is harming employees or people who live nearby, if it's creating unsafe products, or if it's otherwise doing things that infringe on the rights of people, it needs to be held accountable.

Beyond that, no organization can afford to fully ignore the environment in which it operates. "A healthy business, a healthy university, a healthy hospital cannot exist in a sick society," Drucker wrote. "Management has a self-interest in a healthy society, even though the cause of society's sickness is not of management's making." If the public educational system is deteriorating, for instance, corporations have a responsibility to address the problem, in part because their long-term business viability depends on it.

The scandals of the last decade have further reinforced the need for big public companies to be socially responsible. In my book *Revolt in the Boardroom*, which looked at the epidemic of CEO firings in 2005 and 2006, I argued that big public companies are political institutions that need the goodwill of the public to survive and thrive. When they lose that goodwill, as they have in the last decade, they bring all manner of ills upon themselves that can ultimately threaten the viability of their business.

A.G. Lafley, who served as CEO of P&G through most of the first decade of the twenty-first century, is one of the newer breed of business leaders who understands this. In an interview, he explained how his recent predecessors focused on "shareholders," but he tended to talk about "stakeholders." When I asked him to tell me who those stakeholders were, he mentioned his employees, as well as the managers and employees of the thousands of companies P&G sells to, as well as its thousands of suppliers. Stakeholders also included its potential customers in more than 160 countries, and the communities where all of these people live.

By the time he was done, it was difficult for me to imagine anyone on the planet who *wasn't* a P&G stakeholder.

Lee Scott, who ran Walmart during the same decade, was another. Soon after he assumed the top job in the early 2000s, he found himself facing a coordinated campaign from union-financed groups attempting to show Walmart was bad for the workers whom it employed as well as the communities in which its stores were located. Scott went on the offensive, spending much of his tenure as CEO trying to show the world that Walmart was, in effect, paying attention to the Triple Bottom Line: it was not only making money but also creating good jobs for people and working toward a healthier planet.

In talking with CEOs who emphasize corporate social responsibility, I've found another strong common theme: many of them say they do it for their employees.

Think back to chapter 3, "Motivation." Modern workers want to feel good about what they do. And that often translates into wanting to work for a company that does good things. By taking an active role in addressing environmental issues or other social issues, companies are often making an appeal to the people who work for them, or to others whom they may wish to recruit to work for them. Technology companies in particular, which are engaged in a constant competition for talent, say they find workers more eager to work for a company that is socially responsible.

EXECUTIVE PAY

Soaring CEO pay has become a flash point for public anger toward business. And it's no surprise. During the peak years, executives like Richard Fairbank of Capital One could earn as much as $250 million in a single year. Even as the financial crisis took hold in 2008, pay levels only dipped a modest 3.4 percent.

Citigroup's Vikram Pandit, whose bank later had to take fifty billion in taxpayer dollars to survive, earned a total of $38 million that year. Disney's Bob Iger earned $49 million. Motorola's Sanjay Jha earned $104 million.

Defenders said these folks were paid market rates. They say the rise of CEO paychecks roughly tracks the rising market value of the companies they work for. And they note soaring paychecks track those of TV stars or sports stars.

But if executive pay is set by a market, it's a funny market. Compensation consultants that work with companies tend to set pay levels by looking at what everyone else is paying, and then recommending more. Like the children in Lake Wobegon, everyone wants to be above average. The result is a steadily rising elevator. Moreover, when performance plummets, pay often doesn't—or at least it falls at a less precipitous rate.

Moreover, activism by corporate boards has perversely caused pay levels to rise. That's because after a disgruntled board throws out a CEO, they have to find a new one. And all too often, they haven't done the necessary work to prepare for succession inside the company, so they have to bid for one from the outside.

Unhappiness over CEO pay is fueling proposals for government limits on pay, as well as measures allowing stockholders to veto pay packages. Meanwhile, some executives are starting to conclude that lavish pay packages are just bad business. Workers feel alienated by lavish executive pay, and the public—as well as the politicians in Washington—react angrily. Exercising some restraint now may, in the long run, pay off.

ETHICS in Brief

- Managers should not cheat, steal, lie, bribe, or take bribes. But neither should anyone else.
- Stealing from the company is still stealing.
- Business incentives alone aren't enough to ensure an ethical organization. You need to inject morality into your decision making.

Further Reading

Conspiracy of Fools, by Kurt Eichenwald, Broadway Books, 2005. This is the most detailed account of how the culture at Enron went so badly awry. It's long but reads like a thriller.

Value Shift, by Lynn Sharp Paine, McGraw-Hill, 2003. A Harvard professor's guide to putting moral decision making at the center of your organization.

Revolt in the Boardroom, by Alan Murray, Collins, 2007. My look at how the corporate scandals of 2002 dramatically changed the job of the CEO.

In terms of time management, that's something I'm very proud of what I do. . . . I've got a spreadsheet. It's got to budget my time for the year. I budget how much time I'm going to be out of Seattle and in Seattle. I schedule . . . how I'm going to be spending my time—customers, partners, etc. I schedule all of my formal meetings. I budget my free time. I budget free weeks, days, half days periodically. . . . I still have young kids, and I want to be tough about the eighty-five to ninety nights a year I'm scheduled not to be home with them. . . . Then I give the budget allocation to my administrative assistants, they lay it all out, then anybody who asks for time, they say "Steve, this is in budget, or it's out of budget. How do you want us to handle it?"

STEVE BALLMER, *CEO, Microsoft*,
in a video interview for The Wall Street Journal's
Lessons in Leadership series

Chapter **TWELVE**

MANAGING YOURSELF

Business is always personal. It's the most personal thing in
the world.

MICHAEL SCOTT, *The Office*

Throughout this book we've stressed that to succeed as a manager, you
must put your organization's needs above your own. Management is a
higher calling. It requires you to dedicate yourself to a cause greater
than self.

For the new manager, the transition can be especially jarring. Odds
are, you were made manager in part because of your own successes.
You performed splendidly, you surpassed everyone's expectations,
you achieved superior results, you were the office star. *You* deserved
a reward.

Then, all of a sudden, it's not about you anymore.

As a manager, you have to stop thinking about your own success
and start thinking about the group's. You can no longer afford to look at
those around you as competitors, or as potential obstacles on your way
to advancement. Instead, they have become your road to advancement.
Your new job requires you to nurture them, to coach them, to help them
succeed, and ultimately to take satisfaction from their collective success, rather than your own singular success.

To do that, you need to be self-aware, self-confident, secure, grounded. You need to be everything that *The Office*'s Michael Scott, or *Dilbert*'s pointy-headed boss, isn't. Indeed, as you think about the failings of managers around you, you may be tempted to ask: Why did we leave this chapter for last? In many ways, this challenge— managing yourself—is the greatest challenge you face.

As discussed earlier, human beings are unique in their capacity for self-awareness. We can rise above ourselves, analyze our actions, and choose a direction that's different from that dictated by our emotional needs, our gut instincts, our past habits, or our history.

But having the capacity for self-awareness is different from actually being self-aware. And sorting out distinctions between what feels right and what *is* right, and then acting on those distinctions, is a Herculean task. For the manager, the challenge becomes doubly complex. You must constantly ask yourself: Am I doing this because it is right for me? Or because it is right for the organization?

Consider one deceptively simple decision that Allstate Corporation CEO Edward M. Liddy faced after Hurricane Katrina hit New Orleans. Allstate is the second biggest home and auto insurer in the United States, and it had insured about 350,000 homes in Louisiana, Mississippi, and Alabama—the states hit by the hurricane. The company stood to lose many billions of dollars in claims. Moreover, the whole world was watching. How Allstate handled those claims would likely determine not just the company's survival, but also how it would be perceived by its customers and the public for a generation to come.

When the hurricane hit, Liddy cleared his calendar so he could devote all his attention to the developing disaster. He checked to make sure he had enough claims adjusters in the field, that they had places to stay, that their communications were secure, that they had mobile response units in place, and that they had the information and guidance they needed to make quick decisions on the ground.

Then he had to decide: Should he get in a helicopter and fly to the scene of the disaster?

For a politician, a visit to the site of a catastrophe like Katrina can be an opportunity to make a national reputation. Think, for instance, of what the September 11 tragedy did for New York mayor Rudy Giuliani. For the CEO of Allstate, the effect could have been similar. The public's attention was transfixed. If Liddy swooped in to directly supervise insurance operations on the ground, he would have gotten widespread press coverage and could have created a lasting impression in people's minds as a compassionate man of action. Moreover, he could have justified such action by citing the public relations benefits for Allstate.

Liddy was tempted. But in the end, he decided not to go. Why? Because if top management went to New Orleans, he told the *Journal* one week after the hurricane hit, "we would simply be in the way." If he went, he said, his employees would "spend time and energy" on him, "not on rebuilding customers' lives. That's a much more important priority." Visiting New Orleans might have seemed like a good thing for him to do, but it wasn't the right thing for the organization.

Managers face these sorts of decisions every day—sometimes, many times a day. How you handle them is a constant test of your mettle as a manager. Consider these everyday occurrences:

- Your boss praises a project recently completed by your group. Do you: (1) bask in the glory of the moment? Or (2) use it as an opportunity to point out the work of one or two people in your group who made exceptional contributions?
- You have two candidates for a job opening. One is qualified for the job, and particularly known for loyalty. The other is even more qualified, ambitious, and eager to advance in the organization. Whom do you choose?
- One of your subordinates develops a plan that you fully

approve and that later turns out to be flawed. Do you: (1) accept complete responsibility for having approved the plan, or (2) accept responsibility in public but subtly let it be known that your subordinate "let you down."

- You have an employee who has increasingly shown herself to be smarter, faster, more creative and willing to work longer hours than anyone else in your group—including yourself. Do you: (1) constantly look for new ways to showcase her talents, or (2) encourage her to ease up, for fear she may be overshadowing you and her fellow employees.

As these examples show, doing the "right" thing for your organization sometimes requires you to do things that may feel "wrong" for you. To make the right decision, you need to feel secure in your job. But how many of us in today's uncertain business world feel truly secure in our jobs? To do the right thing, you need to be confident that if you take actions in the best interest of the organization, you'll be rewarded in the long run. But how many of us really have that kind of confidence in the people we work for?

You may be the best manager around, but that doesn't mean your boss is. What if he or she chooses to give your job to a more ambitious, and less costly, subordinate? Giving others credit, hiring ambitious employees, accepting responsibility for mistakes others make, or allowing subordinates to shine may all be actions that are good for the organization but that, in the wrong circumstances, could hurt you.

Indeed, good management has at its core a fundamental conflict. The best managers are always striving to create such well-functioning organizations that they become unnecessary. If they succeed, they become redundant. But if they become redundant, then what?

Later in this chapter, we'll provide some practical tips on how good managers can manage bad bosses—a critical survival skill.

Beyond that, we'd encourage you to think of good management as its own reward. In this book, we've tried to teach you how to get the most out of your organization. After that, all we can hope is that the results speak for themselves

CONTROL YOURSELF

As a manager, you will quickly find that many of the instincts and responses that enabled you to succeed in the workplace now need to be suppressed. Particularly as a new manager, you may still be thinking about how to get yourself ahead, instead of your group. Some advice on how to respond:

- Resist the urge to always win. You may have once taken pride in your ability to dominate internal arguments. You mustered all your facts, you argued your points with great vigor, and you beat back opposing points of view. That's one reason you were promoted to manager. But if you continue to take the same argumentative approach with the people you manage, you're likely to find that they quickly lose any incentive to argue back. To encourage debate and a free flow of ideas, you now have to restrain yourself.

- Don't insist on always making good ideas even better. Before you became a manager, you may always have worked to improve the ideas suggested by others. If Joe had a good idea, you might have responded: "I like that, but I think it could be improved by adding x." As a manager, that same comment suddenly carries the emotional impact of a brickbat. You need to be more generous with the praise, and more sparing and thoughtful about the "buts" and "howevers."

- Don't be too judgmental. You may have gotten your promotion because you had a sharp point of view on every issue. But as a manager, you need to encourage others to give their ideas. They won't, if each one is batted down with an instant, sharp response. Again, it's a good idea to practice restraint. Don't make snap judgments about every idea that comes to you, or you'll find they soon stop coming. Likewise, use sarcasm sparingly. As a manager, your sarcastic comments are far more biting than they were before you had management responsibility.

- Avoid comments designed to show how smart or knowledgeable you are. When someone brings you a new idea, don't say "I already knew that," or "I suggested the same thing three years ago."

- Don't speak when angry. This whole section is about controlling yourself. When you are angry, you are, by definition, out of control.

- Don't withhold important information. Information is a form of power, and some managers will dispense it sparingly in hopes of increasing their own power. It's a bad idea, since without that information, your employees will be less effective. As a manager, you should spread information as broadly as you can.

- Don't claim undue credit, or fail to give proper recognition. Your employees will be watching closely to see how you handle these sorts of situations.

- Don't make excuses. In this and many other things, you set an example. If you make excuses for everything that goes wrong, your employees will do the same.

- Be willing to admit mistakes. Every manager makes them. The difference is that the good ones are quick to admit them, correct them, and learn from them.

- Listen. You may have gotten this far on your own talents, and never developed the skill of listening carefully to others. But as a manager, you are now dependent on others. If you don't learn to listen to what they are saying, you will be unable to tap the collective wisdom of your group.

MANAGE YOURSELF

Let's face it: it's harder to evaluate your own strengths and weaknesses than it is those of your employees. But it's no less important. You need to understand where you fit in the organization, what your contributions are, when you are contributing to better performance, and when you are discouraging it. Yet the natural human tendencies toward denial and self-delusion can make that an exceedingly murky task.

If you're lucky, you may have a boss or mentor who can help you see through the haze and offer useful feedback. More often than not, however, you will find you are on your own. As a result, you need to set up your own mechanisms for encouraging useful feedback. A few suggested approaches follow.

First, for this and other reasons, we advocate an open-door policy—or even better, no door at all. The people you work with need to know you are approachable. They should feel comfortable coming in to raise questions, to challenge you, or to deliver bad news. And they need to know that if they walk through that door with bad news, you won't "shoot the messenger." It's fine to get irritated with people who waste your time asking questions that they know, or at least should know, the answer to. But if you show irritation with the bearer of bad news, or with the person who raises questions about decisions you've made or actions you've taken, you are only hurting yourself. By keeping an open door and encouraging people to come in and challenge you, you are ensuring important feedback that helps you stay on top of what's going on in your organization, and also helps you monitor your own performance.

Even with an open-door policy, though, you may find that good feedback is still relatively scarce. That's human nature—people will shy away from challenging their boss, or sugarcoat the messages they deliver. To guard against that, make sure there are one or two people on your team whom you trust, and who will act as your truth tellers. You may not always enjoy what they have to say; but you'll benefit from their counsel.

As a more formal practice, it's also a good idea to do reverse, or "360 degree" performance reviews. Just as you evaluate your employees' performance, you should ask your employees to evaluate yours. If you are worried they won't be honest with you, try asking an intermediary to collect the evaluations on an anonymous basis, and then summarize the key points for you. You're almost certain to learn one or two things you can do to improve your own performance that you wouldn't have discovered on your own.

LEARNING TO DELEGATE

Delegating is one of the most important things you must do as a manager. But for many, it turns out to be one of the most difficult.

Imagine that you find yourself managing a group of people, and that after careful analysis, you come to the conclusion that you are better than any of them at every task the group is asked to take on.

Leave aside for the moment the likelihood that you have either (1) been less than honest with yourself, or (2) have done a poor job building your team. If you truly are better than everyone at everything, what do you do? Do it all yourself?

The answer, of course, is no. If you try to do it yourself, you'll accomplish very little indeed. Instead, you need to understand and employ what economists call the theory of comparative advantage. You need to decide where each employee can contribute the most value they are capable of contributing, relative to the others. And most important, you need to decide where you can contribute most, and focus your efforts there.

Understanding comparative advantage is the key to successful delegation. How often have you seen a manager delegate a task to someone, and then berate the person because the task wasn't done as well as *he* would have done it? How often have you heard managers complain that they are working twenty hours a day, while their employees sit idle, because no one else in the organization can do things right? Such managers have failed to learn the lessons of comparative advantage.

Often failure to delegate hides fear and insecurity. Management is big and amorphous, and it's not always easy to tell whether one is succeeding at it, or failing. As a result, managers are sometimes tempted to regress and do the tasks they know they do well, rather than tackle the bigger, more challenging tasks demanded of them.

But unwillingness to delegate is one of the biggest causes of management failure. You might think you are proving your own value by showing you do everything better than anyone else. In fact, you are demonstrating the opposite.

Here are two things to keep in mind as you consider delegating responsibilities:

1. As a manager, your job is to hold each of your employees to the highest standard he or she can achieve, not to the standard you would achieve if you held that job; and
2. You need to keep in mind, as mentioned above, that your ultimate success is creating an organization in which you are redundant.

Finally, it's useful to remember the words of Admiral Stockdale:

3. **Strange as it sounds, great leaders gain authority by giving it away.**

MANAGING THE BOSS

As we said at the outset of this book, good management, more often than not, is honored in the breach. As a result, the odds are high that at some point during your career, you'll work for a bad manager. That's okay. Good managers can still succeed, even with bad bosses. But simply being a good manager may not be enough to ensure your survival. So in closing, we want to offer you a few tips for handling the boss.

First, who is the boss? That question is not as easy to answer these days as it was in the days of *The Man in the Gray Flannel Suit*. In a highly matrixed organization, you will likely have multiple bosses. Or at least multiple people who think they are your boss. Or more important, multiple people whose opinions will matter when it comes time to evaluate you, compensate you, promote you, etc.

So a good starting point is to make a list of all the people who, in one sense or another, may consider themselves your boss. If you are an entrepreneur, it may be your investors. If you run a nonprofit, it could be your board. If you are in a large organization, there could be a half dozen people to whom you report in one form or another. Make a complete list, in some order of priority.

Step two is to go to each of those bosses for input. Ask them what you can do to help them or to make their jobs easier. Get their advice on how they think you should do your job. You may be surprised by how appreciative they'll be of your questions. If you start by putting your bosses at ease—let them know you're there to make them look better—you'll often find them supportive of you in return.

Step three is to keep all your bosses well informed. In talking with your bosses, be sure to find out how each of them wants to get information from you. Would they like monthly briefings? Would they prefer them in writing or in person? What kind of specific information would they like to see in those briefings? You may have to tailor your reports to suit the different needs of different bosses, but in the long run, it's worth it.

Also, be quick to inform your bosses when your plans go awry. No one likes negative surprises—they can often lead to public humiliation. It's a good policy to try to make certain that any bad information about your organization comes from you first. You may be reluctant to be the bearer of bad tidings, but believe me, it will go over far better if you bear it than if someone else does.

Finally, even in private, don't underestimate or be overly critical of your boss. As you've learned by now, this management stuff isn't easy. Cut the big guy (or gal) a little slack for occasional missteps, in the hope that your employees will do the same for you.

BEING A WOMAN IN THE WORKPLACE

As we mentioned in chapter 4, there are a whole series of workplace behaviors that are more commonly associated with women than with men, and that can undercut women's advancement.

As a manager, it's your responsibility to avoid creating an overly "male" culture that discriminates against those who use such behaviors.

But as a woman, you'd be smart to avoid or downplay these behaviors.

In her book *Nice Girls Don't Get the Corner Office*, Lois Frankel comes up with a list of 101 "unconscious mistakes" that women make that undercut their careers. I'm not going to list them all here, but some are quite telling.

Mistake number one, for instance, is *Pretending It Isn't a Game.* Men tend to approach the workplace as a sporting match, she says, and their goal is to win. Women tend to approach it more like an event—a picnic, a concert, a fund-raiser—where everyone comes together for the day to play nicely. "In our desire to create win-win situations," she writes, "we unknowingly create win-lose ones—where we're the losers."

Frankel speculates that the rise of women's athletics will undercut this difference over time, as more and more women coming into the workplace understand the game.

Speech patterns can be another critical distinction. Frankel advises against couching statements as questions, using minimizing words like "I just . . ." or "It was only . . . ," or excessively apologizing.

And how you look matters, too. Frankel upbraids women for "smiling inappropriately" or avoiding energetic gestures.

BUILDING YOUR OWN BRAND

If you follow all the lessons of this book, will it guarantee you a life of management success?

Well, sorry, but the answer is: no.

Even the very best managers suffer setbacks and failures. And in today's world, even the best-managed organizations hit unexpected brick walls. Moreover, the workplace has become a much less forgiving place than it was two or three decades ago, and job terminations have become far more commonplace. The odds that you'll end your career working for the same organization you started with are close to nil. You should always prepare yourself for change, and be ready to embrace it.

That means it's more important than ever for you to keep your job in perspective. It never has been, and never will be, a replacement for friends and family. You need to devote time and energy to those relationships along your way. They'll likely be far more loyal and lasting than your employer ever will.

You also need to pay attention to developing yourself, so if your current job disappears, you are ready for the challenges of a new one. Think of your life as a continuing education, in which you strive to accumulate skills and experiences that will be useful in the next phase, whatever that may be. Think of yourself as a brand, and you are the brand manager, burnishing the qualities that will increase your value over time.

We'll end this book by giving the last word to the man whose name is still the first word in management: Peter Drucker. He wrote of experiences in his life that taught him to "maintain myself as effective, capable of growth, capable of change—and capable of aging without becoming a prisoner of the past." Here are three of them:

The lesson of Verdi. As a young man, Drucker frequented the opera and was particularly impressed by a performance of *Falstaff*, written by the great nineteenth-century Italian composer Giuseppe Verdi, "with its gaiety, its zest for life, and its incredible vitality."

Then Drucker learned that Verdi had written the opera at the age of eighty. And he came across, and long remembered, these words written by the great composer: "All my life as a musician, I have striven for perfection. It always eluded me. I'm sure I had an obligation to make one more try."

The lesson of Phidias. As he continued his own quest for perfection, Drucker discovered the story of Phidias, considered to be the greatest sculptor of ancient Greece. He was commissioned in 440 B.C. to make statues for the roof of the Parthenon. But when he submitted the bill for his work, the story goes, the city accountant of Athens rejected it. The statues stand on the roof of the temple on the highest hill in Athens and no one can see anything but their fronts, the accountant said. "Yet, you have charged us for sculpturing them in the round, for doing their backsides, which nobody can see."

Phidias responded: "You are wrong. The gods can see them." That, Drucker says, is the argument he's always tried to remember in pursuing his work.

The lessons of journalism. Drucker began his career as a journalist in Frankfurt, Germany, and he loved the work, because in journalism, he was continuously forced to learn about new subjects.

He would use his evenings to study a different subject—history, law, finance, and so on. And he developed a system that he says he adhered to for the rest of his life. Every three or four years, he would pick a new subject—statistics, medieval history, Japanese art—and study it, forcing himself to continuously expand his body of understanding and knowledge.

Successful people, he writes, "build continuous learning into the way they live. . . . They experiment. They are not satisfied with what they did yesterday. The very least they demand of themselves is that they do better, whatever they do, and more often, they demand of themselves that they do it differently."

While this book has been about building great organizations, ultimately it is not organizations, but individuals, who must take on the responsibility for achieving greatness. We hope what you've read here will help in that quest.

MANAGING Yourself in Brief

- As a manager, you need to stop thinking first about your own success and start thinking about the group's.
- Your employees may not be honest with you; as a result, look for ways to get candid feedback on your own performance.
- Your greatest accomplishment would be creating a workplace in which you are unnecessary.
- Keep all of your bosses well informed. Avoid surprises.

Further Reading

Management, by Peter Drucker, Collins, 2008, pp. 479–504. Drucker's writings on managing yourself and managing the boss remain as good as anything written since.

It's Okay to Be the Boss, by Bruce Tulgan, HarperCollins, 2007. A practical guide on how to act as a manager.

Crazy Bosses, by Stanley Bing, Collins, 2008. Read this one just for fun, and to remind yourself that you're not the first person to have a bad boss.

What Got You Here Won't Get You There, by Marhsall Goldsmith with Mark Reiter, Hyperion, 2007. This book looks at how the self-promotional skill that likely helped you get your management job could undercut your performance as a manager.

Nice Girls Don't Get the Corner Office, by Lois P. Frankel, Warner Business Books, 2004. A hundred and one mistakes women make in the workplace—a valuable book for any woman trying to survive and thrive in a "male" workplace.

CONCLUSION

Management is not a science. Don't let anyone tell you otherwise.

One of the great conceits of the twentieth century was that human behavior and human institutions could be analyzed according to the methods of the physical sciences. It was a powerful idea, not without useful insights, and pervaded advanced academic thinking. But in the end, it proved wrongheaded.

That's because the ultimate joy and frustration of human existence is that we don't behave according to ironclad rules of behavior, and that our lives and the institutions we build are imbued with love, hatred, joy, envy, honor, corruption, greed, self-sacrifice—all the traits that make us human. Peter Drucker recognized this long ago, when he parted ways with economists, whom he said "were interested in the behavior of commodities, while I was interested in the behavior of people." Others took longer to recognize this essential difference.

Indeed as the last century ended, there was a pervasive sense of scientific triumph. The cold war had ended, communism had been vanquished, capitalism was spreading throughout the world, and one analyst even dared to title a popular book: *The End of History*. The Internet had conquered distance, collapsed national boundaries, and some dreamers even imagined that it had vanquished the business cycle and would lead to ever-expanding economic growth, carrying the stock market—to cite another popular book title of the time—to *Dow 36,000.*

The first decade of the twenty-first century, however, provided a series of powerful reminders of our essential humanity. The Internet bubble collapsed and left the dreamers nursing their wounds. Then came September 11, and the brazen attack on the World Trade Center by religious fanatics who were happy to sacrifice their own lives in order to kill thousands of anonymous others. Corporate scandals early in the decade provided painful reminders of the prevalence of corruption. Two brutal wars demonstrated human history was far from over. An orgy of mortgage lending topped off by a frenzy of securitization demonstrated how easily hope and greed could overwhelm even the most basic common sense among the smartest of people. And a spectacular financial collapse showed us that even the most sophisticated human systems were inevitably infected with our frailties.

All of this leaves managers with the ultimate challenge. They are artists, not scientists. They must deal with all the complexities and uncertainties of human behavior, and they must do so in a world where technology has accelerated time and eliminated borders and has magnified both the best and the worst traits of society.

In the medium term, it's possible to detect a few trends. Trust in business by the public at large is clearly at a low point and is likely to stay there for some time. Government involvement in the economy, on the retreat for the last quarter of the twentieth century, is clearly on the rise. Financing is likely to be harder to come by in the years ahead, and American consumers, who powered the global economy for decades, will pull in their wallets. Asia will likely continue to rise, and technological change will likely continue to accelerate.

Yet success in the new era won't ultimately require a perfect crystal ball—none of us has one. Rather, it will require institutions that can survive through uncertainty and thrive amid rapid change, and managers who have the humility to know that they don't have all the answers but do have the confidence and willingness and judgment to lead their team to find them.

When we asked members of the *Journal*'s CEO Council to name the best management books they had read, several mentioned Nassim Nicholas Taleb's *The Black Swan*. The book, published in 2007, argues that the most important events in life tend to be those that can neither be foreseen nor predicted—the "black swans" of the title. No amount of knowledge or learning will enable you to see them coming. And thus knowing what you don't know becomes as important as what you do know.

This book has offered some practical advice on how to handle some of the black swans you may encounter as you navigate through the fog. In closing, we'd like to offer some broader advice that we believe will serve any manager well in the years ahead:

Stay flexible. Managers will need a flexible organization, so that it can be repositioned quickly to address new threats and master new challenges. You will have to be prepared to reevaluate your mission, strategy, and goals more frequently than before, in order to adjust to the uncertain and changing environment.

Devour data. Managers will need to have their "ears to the ground" in order to hear changes as they are coming. That means you'll need to seek out fresh sources of information, intelligence, and data. You'll need to follow the example of leaders like A.G. Lafley, former CEO of Procter & Gamble, who required his top executives to go out into the field and talk to the ordinary women who use P&G products.

Be (somewhat) humble. Managers will not be able to assume they know the answer—because more often than not, they won't. You'll need to be willing to hear hard truths from your employees, your customers, your suppliers, and anyone else closer to a changing marketplace than you are.

Communicate. The days of keeping your head down as a manager, focusing on operations instead of external communications, are over. More than ever, managers have to become advocates. Critics will abound, and you'll need to be able to rally the support of your employees, your customers and clients, and a whole array of outside stakeholders to survive and thrive.

Plan for contingencies. It's natural for people to focus on what they know, but as a result, as Taleb says, we "time and time again fail to take into account what we don't know." With rising uncertainty, the advantage goes to those who can imagine the improbable. Keeping cash and other resources on hand for emergencies will also become increasingly important.

Be proactive. If you see a problem coming, don't wait until it hits you . . . by then it will be too late. You will need to be prepared to react quickly.

Insist on candor. To succeed in an uncertain and rapidly changing environment, it's critical that everyone in an organization be brutally honest. There's no time for dealing with the small lies that people routinely use to burnish their own record or avoid offending others. Everyone needs to know exactly where things stand at all times.

Stay involved. At times like the present, no manager can afford to be seen hiding in his or her office. It's important that you be seen out among your employees, in part to give them confidence, and in part to collect necessary intelligence.

Keep your organization flat. It was a good idea before the new era; it's critical now. You can't afford to have layers of bureaucracy between you and the action. That will guarantee that you are too slow to react.

Cross-train your talent. Good managers have been knocking down silos in their organizations for years. But again, what used to be a good practice is now essential. You need people with multiple skills, who aren't qualified for just one narrow task, and who can be redeployed as the situation demands it.

Assess your team. In the current new and unforgiving environment, few organizations can afford to have people who aren't pulling their weight. You need to be constantly reassessing your team, making sure you encourage and promote the best, and dealing quickly with those who aren't contributing.

And finally,

Use your judgment. No team of PhD students building computer-powered mathematical models will ever be a good substitute for common sense. You didn't have to be a rocket scientist to know it wasn't a good idea to make housing loans to people who put no money down, or to waive rules requiring them to document their income, or to make loans with payments that would balloon in two or three years when they couldn't afford the balloon payments. The bankers who survived this crisis weren't the ones with the most sophisticated risk models, but rather the ones who kept their heads.

ACKNOWLEDGMENTS

This book would not have been possible without the help of:

Generations of dedicated *Wall Street Journal* journalists who have created the greatest business news gathering organization ever known;

Robert Thomson, Les Hinton, and Rupert Murdoch, who at a critical point in the history of the *Journal* showed us the value of a culture biased toward action;

My longtime mentor, Paul Steiger, who trained me in the best forms of journalism, and my friend, Marcus Brauchli, who created a way for me to stay at the *Journal*;

My colleagues and teachers in the Senior Executive Program Class of 2005 at the Stanford Graduate School of Business, who gave me my only formal training in management. (They did as well as they could in the brief time allotted and can't be held accountable for this book's shortcomings);

My very skilled editor at HarperCollins; Hollis Heimbouch; my partner at *Wall Street Journal* books, Roe D'Angelo; my colleague Joanne Lublin, who's the best copyeditor I know; and my mother, Catherine Murray, who is still sharper than a tack at (age deleted), and who caught a dozen typos in the final proofs;

My wonderful wife, Lori, and two exceptional children, Lucyann and Amanda, who provide the ultimate motivation for all that I do.

INDEX

MORE BOOKS FROM
THE WALL STREET JOURNAL

THE WALL STREET JOURNAL GUIDE TO THE END OF WALL STREET AS WE KNOW IT
What You Need to Know About the Greatest Financial Crisis of Our Time— and How to Survive It
By Dave Kansas

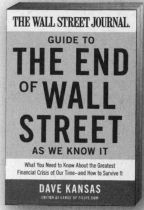

ISBN 978-0-06-178840-6 (paperback)
The definitive resource for Main Street readers who want to make sense of what's happening on Wall Street, and better understand how we got here and what we need to know in the days to come.

THE WALL STREET JOURNAL GUIDE TO POWER TRAVEL
How to Arrive with Your Dignity, Sanity, and Wallet Intact
By Scott McCartney

ISBN 978-0-06-168871-3 (paperback)
Imagine a world without late planes, missed connections, lost luggage, bumped passengers, cramped seating, high fares, and security lines. From *The Wall Street Journal* "Middle Seat" columnist, this book shows readers how to secure ease, civility, comfort, and good deals on the road.

THE WALL STREET JOURNAL ESSENTIAL GUIDE TO MANAGEMENT
Lasting Lessons from the Best Leadership Minds of Our Time
By Alan Murray

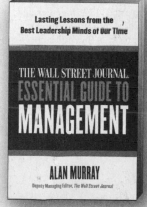

ISBN 978-0-06-184033-3 (paperback)
The ultimate guide on how to be a successful manager at any level in all kinds of industries and organizations. Here readers will find the best information on management practices summarized in one place, in a simple, clear, and useful way.

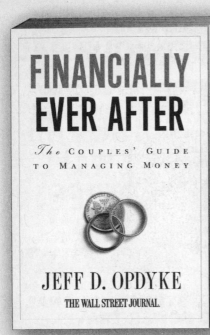

FINANCIALLY EVER AFTER
The Couples' Guide to Managing Money
By Jeff D. Opdyke

ISBN 978-0-06-135818-0 (paperback)

Financially Ever After is every couple's manual for managing both the real dollars and the real emotions of personal finance that course through every relationship after the "I do's" are done.

The Wall Street Journal's long-time syndicated Love & Money columnist covers such topics as budgeting, joint vs. individual accounts, confronting debt, making major purchases, mortgages, employment, children, and even engagement rings. This book lays the groundwork for a financially successful marriage.

PIGGYBANKING
Preparing Your Financial Life for Kids and Your Kids for a Financial Life
By Jeff D. Opdyke

ISBN 978-0-06-135819-7 (paperback)

When couples are planning their financial lives together, few questions are as significant as how to afford a family. To help couples meet this challenge, veteran *Wall Street Journal* personal finance writer Jeff Opdyke lays out everything they need to do to prepare for the expense of having kids, and how to handle the obligation of teaching their kids about money. *Piggybanking* is truly the must-have financial guide all parents need in order to create a sound financial life for their family.

ALSO FROM
ALAN MURRAY

The imperial CEO is gone. In its place is a new, and often messy, system of board rule...

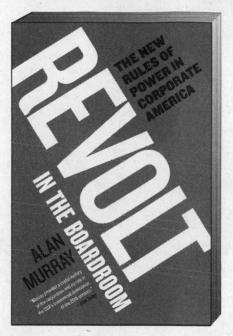

REVOLT IN THE BOARDROOM
The New Rules of Power in Corporate America

Noted *Wall Street Journal* editor and columnist Alan Murray uncovers the tectonic power shift in the corporate C-suite over the last five years—a shift in the underpinnings of power in corporate America that has made the life and tenure of today's CEO nasty, brutish, and short. This book tells the tumultuous inside story of this power shift while examining what caused it and exploring what it means for the future of American business.

"Draw[s] insight from even the best-known corporate blow-ups." —*BusinessWeek*

ISBN 978-0-06-088248-8 (paperback)